The Original

Summer Bridge Activities™

Bridging Grades Fifth to Sixth

Caution: Exercise activities may require adult supervision. Before beginning any exercise activity, consult a physician. Written parental permission is suggested for those using this book in group situations. Children should always warm up prior to beginning any exercise activity and should stop immediately if they feel any discomfort during exercise.

Caution: Before beginning any food activity, ask parents' permission and inquire about the child's food allergies and religious or other food restrictions.

Caution: Nature activities may require adult supervision. Before beginning any nature activity, ask parents' permission and inquire about the child's plant and animal allergies. Remind the child not to touch plants or animals during the activity without adult supervision.

Caution: Before beginning any balloon activity, ask parents about possible latex allergies. Also, remember that uninflated or popped balloons may present a choking hazard.

The authors and publisher are not responsible or liable for any injury that may result from performing the exercises or activities in this book.

Credits

Series Creator: Michele D. Van Leeuwen

Content Editor: Ashley Anderson

Copy Editors: Carrie Fox, Ginny Swinson

Layout and Cover Design: Chasity Rice

Cover Illustration: Robbie Short

ISBN 978-1-60418-822-6

Table of Contents

...ow that many children experience learning loss when they do not engage ...ational activities during the summer? This means that some of what they have ...n time learning over the preceding school year evaporates during the summer ...onths. However, summer learning loss is something that you can help prevent. Below are a few suggestions for fun and engaging activities that can help children maintain and grow their academic skills during the summer.

- Read with your child every day. Visit your local library together and select books on subjects that interest your child.

- Ask your child's teacher to recommend books for summer reading.

- Explore parks, nature preserves, museums, and cultural centers.

- Consider every day as a day full of teachable moments. Measuring ingredients for recipes and reviewing maps before a car trip are ways to learn or reinforce skills.

- Each day, set goals for your child to accomplish. For example, complete five math problems or read one section or chapter in a book.

- Encourage your child to complete the activities in books such as Summer Bridge Activities™ to help bridge the summer learning gap.

To learn more about summer learning loss and summer learning programs, visit *www.summerlearning.org.*

Have a memorable summer!

Ron Fairchild

CEO, National Summer Learning Association

About Summer Bridge Activities™

Summer Bridge Activities™: Bridging Grades Fifth to Sixth prepares your rising sixth grade for a successful school year. The activities in this book are designed to review the skills that your child mastered in fifth grade, preview the skills that he or she will learn in sixth grade, and help prevent summer learning loss. No matter how wonderful your child's classroom experiences are, your involvement outside of the classroom is crucial to his or her academic success. Together with *Summer Bridge Activities™: Bridging Grades Fifth to Sixth*, you can fill the summer months with learning experiences that will deepen and enrich your child's knowledge and prepare your child for the upcoming school year.

Summer Bridge Activities™ is the original workbook series developed to help parents support their children academically during the summer months. While many other summer workbook series are available, Summer Bridge Activities™ continues to be the series that teachers recommend most.

The three sections in this workbook correspond to the three months of traditional summer vacation. Each section begins with a goal-setting activity, a word list, and information about the fitness and character development activities located throughout the section.

To achieve maximum results, your child should complete two activity pages each day. Activities cover a range of subjects, including reading comprehension, grammar, writing, multiplication and division, fractions, algebra, geometry, science, and social studies. These age-appropriate activities are presented in a fun and creative way to challenge and engage your child. Each activity page is numbered by day.

Bonus extension activities that encourage outdoor learning, science experiments, and social studies exercises are located at the end of each section. Complete these activities with your child throughout each month as time allows.

An answer key located at the end of the book allows you to check your child's work. Flash cards help reinforce basic skills, and a certificate of completion will help you and your child celebrate his or her summer learning success!

	Addition & Subtraction	Algebra	Capitalization & Punctuation	Character Development	Critical Thinking	Data Analysis	Decimals, Fractions, & Percentages	Fitness	Geometry & Measurement	Grammar	Language Arts	Multiplication & Division	Numbers & Estimation	Parts of Speech	Problem Solving	Reading Comprehension	Science	Sentence Structure & Types	Social Studies	Vocabulary & Spelling	Writing
1	★										★	★		★			★				
2													★	★					★		
3													★	★		★					
4											★		★	★	★						★
5							★				★		★								
6														★	★	★					
7					★							★		★						★	
8											★			★	★		★				
9											★			★		★					
10				★							★	★		★							
11											★	★		★						★	
12											★			★						★	★
13											★			★		★					
14											★				★					★	★
15							★				★	★		★							
16		★												★		★					
17		★									★			★							
18						★					★			★			★				
19						★								★		★					
20						★					★			★							
					★						**BONUS PAGES!**						★		★	★	★
1						★					★			★		★					
2						★					★			★		★					
3						★					★			★					★		
4						★		★			★			★							
5						★					★			★		★					
6						★					★			★							★
7				★	★						★							★			
8											★					★		★			
9				★	★									★				★			
10										★	★	★					★				
11	★									★		★		★		★					

Skills Matrix

Day	Addition & Subtraction	Algebra	Capitalization & Punctuation	Character Development	Critical Thinking	Data Analysis	Decimals, Fractions, & Percentages	Fitness	Geometry & Measurement	Grammar	Language Arts	Multiplication & Division	Numbers & Estimation	Parts of Speech	Problem Solving	Reading Comprehension	Science	Sentence Structure & Types	Social Studies	Vocabulary & Spelling	Writing
12										★	★	★									★
13								★		★	★				★						
14		★								★						★					
15		★									★			★			★				
16		★									★			★		★					
17		★												★		★					
18									★		★						★	★			
19			★						★		★										★
20			★						★							★					
						★			★		**BONUS PAGES!**						★		★		
1		★							★		★					★					
2		★							★		★										★
3		★							★							★					
4		★						★	★											★	
5		★				★			★		★										
6									★				★			★					
7									★	★	★										
8									★	★						★					★
9		★							★							★					
10		★							★		★						★				
11						★								★					★	★	
12						★										★				★	
13			★			★					★									★	
14						★					★						★	★			
15						★										★		★			
16		★				★					★					★				★	
17						★		★			★							★			
18						★				★						★					
19									★		★			★							★
20											★		★	★			★				
						★					**BONUS PAGES!**		★				★		★		★

Encouraging Summer Reading

Literacy is the single most important skill that your child needs to be successful in school. The following list includes ideas of ways that you can help your child discover the great adventures of reading!

- Establish a time for reading each day. Ask your child about what he or she is reading. Try to relate the material to an event that is happening this summer or to another book or story.

- Let your child see you reading for enjoyment. Talk about the great things that you discover when you read.

- Create a summer reading list. Choose books from the reading list (pages ix–x) or head to the library and explore the shelves. A general rule for selecting books at the appropriate reading level is to choose a page and ask your child to read it aloud. If he or she does not know more than five words on the page, the book may be too difficult.

- Read newspaper and magazine articles, recipes, menus, and maps on a daily basis to show your child the importance of reading.

- Find books that relate to your child's experiences. For example, if you are going camping, find a book about camping. This will help your child develop new interests.

- Visit the library each week. Let your child choose his or her own books, but do not hesitate to ask your librarian for suggestions. Often, librarians can recommend books based on what your child enjoyed in the past.

- Make up stories. This is especially fun to do in the car, on camping trips, or while waiting at the airport. Encourage your child to tell a story with a beginning, a middle, and an end. Or, have your child start a story and let other family members build on it.

- Encourage your child to join a summer reading club at the library or a local bookstore. Your child may enjoy talking to other children about the books that he or she has read.

Summer Reading List

The summer reading list includes fiction and nonfiction titles. Experts recommend that fifth- and sixth-grade students read for at least 30 minutes each day. After your child reads, ask questions about the story to reinforce comprehension.

Decide on an amount of daily reading time for each month. You may want to write the time on the Monthly Goals page at the beginning of each section.

Fiction

Atwater, Richard and Florence
Mr. Popper's Penguins

Avi
Windcatcher

Babbitt, Natalie
Tuck Everlasting

Banks, Lynne Reid
The Indian in the Cupboard

Barshaw, Ruth McNally
Ellie McDoodle: New Kid in School

Blume, Judy
Freckle Juice

Brink, Carol Ryrie
Caddie Woodlawn

Brittain, Bill
The Wish Giver: A Tale of Coven Tree

Burnett, Frances Hodgson
The Secret Garden

Butterworth, Oliver
The Enormous Egg

Cleary, Beverly
Dear Mr. Henshaw

Clements, Andrew
Frindle
Lunch Money
No Talking

Colfer, Eion
Artemis Fowl

Collins, Suzanne
Gregor the Overlander

Conrad, Pam
Pedro's Journal: A Voyage with Christopher Columbus August 3, 1492–February 14, 1493

Dahl, Roald
Charlie and the Great Glass Elevator
Matilda

DiCamillo, Kate
The Tale of Despereaux

Fitzhugh, Louise
Harriet the Spy

Gardiner, John Reynolds
Stone Fox

George, Jean Craighead
My Side of the Mountain

Harper, Charise Mericle
Just Grace

Summer Reading List (continued)

Fiction (continued)

Horowitz, Anthony
Stormbreaker: The Graphic Novel
    adapted by Antony Johnston

Kinney, Jeff
Diary of a Wimpy Kid

MacLachlan, Patricia
Sarah, Plain and Tall

Naylor, Phyllis Reynolds
Shiloh

Paterson, Katherine
Bridge to Terabithia
The Great Gilly Hopkins

Polacco, Patricia
Pink and Say

Rowling, J. K.
Harry Potter and the Sorcerer's Stone

Ryan, Pam Muñoz
Esperanza Rising

Sacher, Louis
Holes

Salisbury, Graham
Under the Blood-Red Sun

Selden, George
The Cricket in Times Square

Smith, Jeff
Bone

Snicket, Lemony
The Bad Beginning, or Orphans!

Spinelli, Jerry
Maniac Magee

Wilder, Laura Ingalls
Little House on the Prairie

Nonfiction

Colbert, David
Thomas Edison

Curlee, Lynn
Trains

Freedman, Russell
Out of Darkness: The Story of Louis Braille

Hall, Julie
A Hot Planet Needs Cool Kids:
    Understanding Climate Change and
    What You Can Do About It

Montgomery, Sy
Quest for the Tree Kangaroo: An Expedition
    to the Cloud Forest of New Guinea

Old, Wendie C.
To Fly: The Story of the Wright Brothers

Ryan, Pam Muñoz
When Marian Sang

St. George, Judith
So You Want to Be an Explorer?

Webb, Sophie
My Season with Penguins:
    An Antarctic Journal

Wick, Walter
A Drop of Water

x

Monthly Goals

A goal is something that you want to accomplish and must work toward. Sometimes, reaching a goal can be difficult.

Think of three goals to set for yourself this month. For example, you may want to exercise for 30 minutes each day. Write your goals on the lines. Post them someplace visible, where you will see them every day.

Draw a line through each goal as you meet it. Feel proud that you have met your goals and set new ones to continue to challenge yourself.

1. _____

2. _____

3. _____

Word List

The following words are used in this section. Use a dictionary to look up each word that you do not know. Then, write three sentences. Use a word from the word list in each sentence.

biome	physician
collide	porous
famished	sensible
fantasy	slogan
geyser	superb

1. _____
_____

2. _____
_____

3. _____
_____

Introduction to Flexibility

This section includes fitness and character development activities that focus on flexibility. These activities are designed to get you moving and thinking about building your physical fitness and your character.

Physical Flexibility

To the average person, *flexibility* means being able to accomplish everyday physical tasks easily, like bending to tie a shoe. These everyday tasks can be difficult for people whose muscles and joints have not been used and stretched regularly.

Proper stretching allows muscles and joints to move through their full range of motion, which is important for good flexibility. There are many ways that you stretch every day without realizing it. When you reach for a dropped pencil or a box of cereal on the top shelf, you are stretching your muscles. Flexibility is important to your health and growth, so challenge yourself to improve your flexibility. Simple stretches and activities, such as yoga and tai chi, can improve your flexibility. Set a stretching goal for the summer, such as practicing daily until you can touch your toes.

Flexibility of Character

While it is important to have a flexible body, it is also important to be mentally flexible. Being mentally flexible means being open-minded to change. It can be disappointing when things do not go your way, but this is a normal reaction. Think of a time when unforeseen circumstances ruined your plans. Maybe your mother had to work one weekend, and you could not go to a baseball game with friends because you needed to babysit a younger sibling. How did you deal with this situation?

A large part of being mentally flexible is realizing that there will be situations in life in which unforeseen things happen. Often, it is how you react to the circumstances that affects the outcome. Arm yourself with tools to be flexible, such as having realistic expectations, brainstorming solutions to make a disappointing situation better, and looking for good things that may have resulted from the initial disappointment.

Mental flexibility can take many forms. For example, being fair, respecting the differences of other people, and being compassionate are ways that you can practice mental flexibility. In difficult situations, remind yourself to be flexible, and you will reap the benefits of this important character trait.

Solve each problem.

1. 793 × 27 = _____

2. 483 × 175 = _____

3. 7,136 ÷ 8 = _____

4. 763,947 − 244,398 = _____

5. 8)9,696 = _____

6. 45)29,745 = _____

7. 63,459 − 21,365 = _____

8. $678.14 + $990.27 = _____

9. 569,040 ÷ 8 = _____

10. 573 + 4,935 + 7,340 = _____

Write each noun from the word bank under the correct heading.

athlete	shoe	canyon	courage	courtyard
diver	plate	hilltop	joy	kindness
luck	manager	mountain	napkin	owner
pillow	senator	trust	valley	ribbon

Person	**Place**	**Thing**	**Idea**
_____	_____	_____	_____
_____	_____	_____	_____
_____	_____	_____	_____
_____	_____	_____	_____
_____	_____	_____	_____

DAY 1

Add a prefix to each base word to make a new word. Use *mis-*, *re-*, *un-*, *non-*, **or** *pre-*.

EXAMPLE:

view _preview, review_

11. name _____

12. read _____

13. heat _____

14. sure _____

15. treat _____

16. fit _____

17. turn _____

18. call _____

19. stop _____

20. place _____

Match the name of each type of scientific measuring device with the situation in which it would be used.

21. _____ time elapsing during a timed lab test

22. _____ the container in which 100 cc of water would be heated to 100°C

23. _____ accurately measure the volume of a liquid

24. _____ the distance between two objects on a table

25. _____ the angle of incline on a ramp

26. _____ the transfer of a very small amount of water between two test tubes

27. _____ the weight of an unknown solid

28. _____ the temperature of a liquid

A. thermometer

B. graduated cylinder

C. digital scale

D. beaker

E. stopwatch

F. pipette

G. protractor

H. meterstick

FACTOID: Although people in Las Vegas live in the Mojave Desert, they use more water per day than any other city in the world.

Write each number in standard form.

1. 2,000,000 + 600,000 + 80,000 + 5,000 + 300 + 20 + 2 _____

2. 900,000 + 10,000 + 400 + 70 + 8 _____

3. 20,000,000 + 3,000,000 + 400,000 + 9,000 + 30 + 6 _____

4. 1,000,000 + 300,000 + 40,000 + 2,000 + 100 + 10 + 1 _____

5. 400,000 + 5,000 + 200 + 30 + 4 _____

6. 10,000,000 + 6,000,000 + 50,000 + 3,000 + 200 + 40 + 5 _____

Write each number in expanded form.

EXAMPLE:

72,584,361 _70,000,000 + 2,000,000 + 500,000 + 80,000 + 4,000 + 300 + 60 + 1_

7. 37,126,489 _____

_____

8. 56,487,320,960 _____

_____

Write S if the noun is singular, P if it is plural, or C if it is collective.

9.	_____ audience		10.	_____ flock	
11.	_____ crowd		12.	_____ crew	
13.	_____ government		14.	_____ sandwiches	
15.	_____ biscuits		16.	_____ stack	
17.	_____ icicle		18.	_____ hydrants	
19.	_____ valley		20.	_____ morsel	
21.	_____ errand		22.	_____ family	
23.	_____ committee		24.	_____ songs	

DAY 2

Circle the word that correctly completes each sentence.

25. One day, Wendy and Wilma decided to go (camp, camping, camped).

26. They (pack, packing, packed) everything they needed in their truck.

27. Then, they went to (hunt, hunting, hunted) for a good place to camp.

28. After looking for a long time, they (pick, picking, picked) a great campsite.

29. (Park, Parking, Parked) the truck was tricky because the ground was slippery.

30. Wendy went (splash, splashing, splashed) through a big puddle.

Use an atlas to find the major North American city that is closest to each latitude and longitude.

31. 61°N, 150°W _____

32. 34°N, 118°W _____

33. 39°N, 95°W _____

34. 30°N, 90°W _____

35. 42°N, 83°W _____

36. 45°N, 76°W _____

37. 35°N, 107°W _____

38. 41°N, 74°W _____

39. 39°N, 82°W _____

40. 51°N, 114°W _____

 FITNESS FLASH: Practice a V-sit. Stretch five times.

* See page ii.

Round each addend to the largest place value. Then, estimate each sum.

EXAMPLE:

711,393 + 202,501 = _700,000 + 200,000 = 900,000_

1. 45 + 32 = _____

2. 91 + 57 = _____

3. 389 + 412 = _____

4. 222 + 387 = _____

5. 948 + 511 = _____

6. 2,735 + 4,960 = _____

7. 10,365 + 3,910 = _____

8. 22,100 + 30,439 = _____

9. 110,345 + 7,630 = _____

10. 23,547 + 12,746 = _____

Cross out the plural or possessive noun in each sentence. Then, write the word correctly. If the word is already correct, write _correct_.

11. All of the news reporter's decided to stay at the Brookgreen Inn.

_____

12. Ten driver's went out on the job this morning, but only nine returned.

_____

13. One drivers truck was stuck in a huge snowdrift.

_____

14. The announcer's voice sounded awful this morning.

_____

15. Many authors attended a convention to come up with new ideas for books.

_____

16. The organizer's of this party can be proud of themselves.

_____

DAY 3

Read the passage. Then, answer the questions.

The Eagle Has Landed

American astronauts Neil Armstrong and Buzz Aldrin were the first people to walk on the moon. Their Lunar Module (LM) left Apollo 11 at 1:45 P.M. on July 20, 1969. "The Eagle has wings," Armstrong stated. At 3:46 P.M., the LM emerged from behind the moon. It was at an altitude of about 20 miles (32.2 km) from the moon. The astronauts had to make the all-important, final decision of whether to remain in orbit or to descend to the lunar surface.

At approximately 4:07 P.M., Armstrong pressed the button marked "Proceed." But, the computer-controlled guidance system was about to take Aldrin and Armstrong into a football-field-sized crater filled with big boulders and rocks. With only precious seconds to spare, Armstrong took manual control of the spacecraft. He found a clear area amid the menacing rock field below. "Houston," Armstrong radioed, "Tranquility base here. The Eagle has landed."

Armstrong was the first human being to set foot on the moon. As his left foot touched the lunar surface to take the first step, he spoke the now famous words, "That's one small step for man, one giant leap for mankind."

17.   What was Armstrong referring to when he said, "The Eagle has landed"?

_____

18.   The word *lunar* is used several times in the passage. What is another word

for *lunar*? _____

19.   What did the "all-important, final decision" mean to the astronauts? _____

_____

20.   What was the significance of this mission to humankind? _____

_____

21.   What does this passage tell you about the type of men Armstrong and Aldrin

were when they made this journey? _____

_____

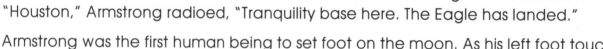
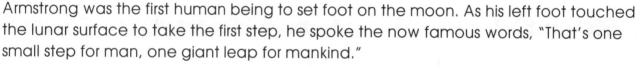
FACTOID: The average temperature on Jupiter is -234°F (-148°C).

Estimate each sum or difference. Then, solve each problem to find the actual sum or difference.

1.　8,666
　　+ 9,346

Estimate: _____

Actual: _____

2.　7,543
　　+ 2,396

Estimate: _____

Actual: _____

3.　47,267
　　+ 55,085

Estimate: _____

Actual: _____

4.　28,790
　　+ 83,964

Estimate: _____

Actual: _____

5.　5,394
　　− 2,587

Estimate: _____

Actual: _____

6.　3,368
　　− 2,139

Estimate: _____

Actual: _____

7.　69,293
　　− 22,887

Estimate: _____

Actual: _____

8.　125,394
　　− 69,831

Estimate: _____

Actual: _____

9.　If each person in the United States drinks 42 gallons of milk per year and each gallon costs $3.98, how much would each person spend on milk per year?

Estimate: _____

Actual: _____

10.　Gloria bought 25 pairs of socks at $5.80 a pair. If her mother gave her $500, would she have enough money left to buy 6 pairs of shoes at $30 a pair?

Estimate: _____

Actual: _____

Circle the noun(s) that correctly completes each sentence.

11.　The (teachers', teachers) conference was held in San Diego, California.

12.　That (mountain, mountains) peak is too difficult for me to climb.

13.　We saw a herd of (deer, deers) along the side of the road.

14.　Why do (goose, geese) have webbed (foot, feet)?

15.　My father caught 10 rainbow (trout, trouts) yesterday.

16.　The nurse took the pulses of the (patient, patients).

17.　When I cannot fall asleep, I count (sheep, sheeps).

18.　My mother bought two pairs of (scissor, scissors).

DAY 4

Add a prefix, suffix, or both to each base word.

19. _____ agree

20. _____ placed

21. _____ respect _____

22. _____ capable

23. avoid _____

24. _____ change

25. delay _____

26. _____ number _____

27. loyal _____

28. hazard _____

29. care _____

30. _____ depend _____

31. _____ necessary

32. thank _____

33. thought _____

34. marvel _____

35. _____ verb

36. _____ mature

37. _____ comfort _____

38. _____ plant

39. act _____

A limerick is a humorous five line poem with a set rhyme scheme, AABBA. This means that the first, second, and fifth lines rhyme and the third and fourth lines rhyme. Write a limerick about your summer vacation.

_____

_____

_____

_____

_____

_____

_____

_____

FITNESS FLASH: Touch your toes 10 times.

* See page ii.

Estimate each sum, difference, product, or quotient. Then, solve each problem to find the actual solution.

1.
$$\begin{array}{r} 6,525 \\ 3,910 \\ + 2,335 \end{array}$$

Estimate: _____

Actual: _____

2.
$$\begin{array}{r} 1,236 \\ 4,253 \\ + 7,237 \end{array}$$

Estimate: _____

Actual: _____

3.
$$\begin{array}{r} 365,244 \\ - 79,087 \end{array}$$

Estimate: _____

Actual: _____

4.
$$\begin{array}{r} 866,533 \\ - 278,184 \end{array}$$

Estimate: _____

Actual: _____

5.
$$\begin{array}{r} 533 \\ \times \ 24 \end{array}$$

Estimate: _____

Actual: _____

6.
$$\begin{array}{r} 975 \\ \times \ 53 \end{array}$$

Estimate: _____

Actual: _____

7. $24\overline{)164}$

Estimate: _____

Actual: _____

8. $80\overline{)286}$

Estimate: _____

Actual: _____

A pronoun that is part of the subject of a sentence is called a subject pronoun. A pronoun that is not part of the subject is an object pronoun. Write *SP* if the underlined pronoun is a subject pronoun. Write *OP* if it is an object pronoun.

9. _____ The funny story made <u>us</u> laugh.

10. _____ Did <u>they</u> fly or take the train home?

11. _____ Ted held the trophy in front of McCall and <u>her</u>.

12. _____ <u>We</u> are going to Maine this summer.

13. _____ Will <u>we</u> see any sharks at Sea Life Park?

14. _____ Are <u>you</u> a cousin of Hal Tomyn?

15. _____ Denise and <u>I</u> went ice-skating with her family.

16. _____ The dog found <u>it</u> under the kitchen table.

17. _____ Do not give <u>her</u> the present until noon.

18. _____ <u>I</u> bought blue gym shoes this year because I like them.

DAY 5

Study the list of prefixes and suffixes and their meanings. Then, write the meaning of each word.

Prefixes		Suffixes	
re-	back or again	**-ment**	the act, result, or product of
dis-	away, apart, or the opposite of	**-ish**	of or belonging to; like or about
un-	opposite, not, or lack of	**-less**	without or not
pre-	before		

19. punishment _____

20. disappear _____

21. presoak _____

22. rewind _____

23. colorless _____

24. precooked _____

25. unsure _____

26. brownish _____

Balloon Ballet

How graceful are you? Ballet dancers are known to be very strong yet graceful. Their movements are flowing, and they are very flexible. Practicing a graceful walk across the floor like a ballet dancer helps stress good posture. Inflate a balloon and place it on your head. Without looking down, walk on the balls of your feet with your arms above your head. If you can make it several steps without dropping the balloon, you are practicing graceful control.

CHARACTER CHECK: Think of a game you like to play. Write a song, story, or poem promoting fairness in playing the game.

* See page ii.

Solve each word problem. Then, write the name of the operation you used to solve the problem.

1. You can make 36 ice-cream cones from one gallon of ice cream. If you have 12 one-gallon ice-cream containers, how many cones will you need in order to use all of the ice cream? _____

2. Mrs. Stone hand-dipped 425 chocolates during the first part of May, 592 in the middle of May, and 143 during the last part of May. How many chocolates did she make in May? _____

3. Farmer Tim sold 4,987 pounds of potatoes last year and 12,709 pounds this year. How many more pounds of potatoes did he sell this year than last year?

   _____

4. Denim shorts sell for $27.59 a pair at Lornet Department Store. A pair of regular denim jeans sells for $12.18 more than the denim shorts. How much do the store's regular denim jeans cost? _____

Write *I* or *me* to correctly complete each sentence.

EXAMPLE: She and ____*I*____ baked a cake.

5. Mom and _____ went to the store.

6. Will you come to see Ken and _____?

7. Ann Marie and _____ ate our lunches outside.

8. The gift was sent by Aunt Jean and _____.

Circle the possessive pronoun that correctly completes each sentence.

9. (Her, hers) handwriting is very neat.

10. The prize is (his, our).

11. (My, Mine) uncle, Clint, is coming for a visit.

12. The book you loaned to Leza was (my, mine).

DAY 6

Read the passage. Then, answer the questions.

Biomes of Canada

Canada has many different **biomes**, or ecosystems. Some of the southern provinces are covered in grasslands. The Hudson Plains, near Hudson Bay, contain one-quarter of Earth's wetlands, which attract many migrating birds. Much of southern Canada is covered by the Boreal Shield, which includes forests and rivers that were once used for fur trade. Far northern Canada is covered by tundra, which contains permanently frozen ground called permafrost. Much of western Canada is within a mountain biome. The far southeastern provinces are in the Atlantic Maritime biome. Maritime refers to the sea. This area receives heavy rainfall because it is near the Atlantic Ocean. Along Canada's border with the U.S. state of Alaska lie temperate rain forests. Because this area is near the Pacific Ocean, its climate is very mild. The smallest biome, a temperate deciduous forest, contains half of Canada's population and the cities of Toronto and Montreal.

13. What is the main idea of this passage?
    A. Some biomes are mountainous, and others have grasslands.
    B. Many people live in Toronto and Montreal.
    C. Canada has a variety of climates and landscapes.

14. What is a biome? _____

15. Name three biomes that can be found in Canada. _____
    _____

16. What is permanently frozen ground called? _____

17. Why does the Atlantic Maritime biome have heavy rainfall? _____
    _____

18. Which area in Canada contains one-quarter of Earth's wetlands?
    _____

19. What does the term *maritime* refer to? _____

FACTOID: There are more than 1.2 billion teenagers in the world.

Find each quotient.

1. 8)231

2. 5)3,305

3. 75)92,835

4. 4)394

5. 75)675

6. 40)73,847

7. 9)894

8. 70)5,824

Circle the possessive pronoun that correctly completes each sentence.

EXAMPLE:

Maggie collects books, and she likes (her, she) old books best.

9. Ty said that (he, his) parents also collect books.

10. Emily washed (her, hers) hair.

11. I asked (my, mine) sister to give me a ride home.

12. The cat bathed (hers, her) kittens.

13. The girls made lunch for (their, theirs) family.

14. "Craig, please write (yours, your) phone number on the sign-up sheet."

Circle the article(s) that correctly completes each sentence.

15. Was that (a, an, the) alligator or (a, an) crocodile that we saw back there?

16. The student gave her teacher (a, an) crisp, red apple.

17. I saw (a, an) excited child playing with (a, an) fluffy kitten.

18. After (a, an) rainstorm, (a, an, the) sun glistens on (a, an, the) puddles.

19. If March comes in like (a, an, the) lion, it should go out like (a, an, the) lamb.

DAY 7

Write the letter of each definition next to the correct word.

20. _____ geyser
21. _____ advice
22. _____ generate
23. _____ slogan
24. _____ pencil
25. _____ regulate
26. _____ collide
27. _____ gelatin
28. _____ surgery
29. _____ against

A. not in favor of
B. writing instrument
C. produce
D. control
E. operation
F. make hard contact
G. hot spring
H. motto
I. recommendation
J. jellylike substance

There are four trees in the park. The ages of the trees are 18 years, 27 years, 45 years, and 48 years. Use the clues and the table below to find the age of each tree.

- The maple tree is planted beside the oldest tree.
- The pine tree is not the youngest tree.
- The oldest tree has the shortest name.
- The youngest tree is planted across from the maple tree.
- The second youngest tree never has leaves.

	18 years	27 years	45 years	48 years
30. Maple				
31. Pine				
32. Birch				
33. Oak				

FITNESS FLASH: Do arm circles for 30 seconds.

* See page ii.

Cross out the unnecessary information. Then, solve each word problem.

1. The students at Franklin Elementary School are going on a field trip to the Museum of Natural History. On Wednesday, 3,068 students are going, and 2,864 are going on Thursday. Mr. Rand, the principal, wants to order special school name tags that come in packages of 1,000. Each package costs $5.25. How many packages does Mr. Rand need to order? _____

2. Josiah has a pet turtle that eats 5 carrots a week. He also has a pet frog. If carrots cost $0.25 each, how much does it cost Josiah each week to feed his turtle? _____

3. Andy's dad is boiling 2 quarts of water on the stove. He is also baking 5 rolls in the oven. He will use 1 pint of the boiling water for his tea. How many pints of boiling water will he have left to use for his soup? _____

Circle the action verbs. Underline the linking verbs.

walk	seem	is	cry	became
sound	wore	sneezed	become	blew
call	being	read	built	clapped
dance	will	eat	have been	watched
are	gather	cheer	was	wants
be	were	am	speak	have
sit	throw	meowing	has	mopped
caught	jump	barking	carried	had
been	won	selling	has had	hit
honked	dive	climbs	bake	helped
smell	rolled	skiing	wash	carried
plays	wiggled	paint	practice	fed

DAY 8

Write a word from the word bank to complete each sentence.

| allergies | conduct | inlets | frank | stethoscope |
| suspicious | knead | subscribe | margin | owes |

4. All of the _____ around the lake were crowded with boats.

5. The doctor listened to my heart through the _____.

6. The night watchman became _____ of the parked car.

7. We _____ to at least four newspapers.

8. Did you leave a _____ on each side of your paper?

9. Ted always _____ someone money.

10. She was _____ in telling me that the movie was too long.

11. Use both hands when you _____ the bread dough.

12. Three of my classmates have food _____.

13. Toby's _____ at the recital was extremely good.

Matter exists in three states: solid, liquid, and gas. Write each word from the word bank under the correct heading.

| air | box | dust | helium | hydrogen | ice |
| juice | lava | milk | oxygen | rock | water |

Solid	Liquid	Gas
_____	_____	_____
_____	_____	_____
_____	_____	_____
_____	_____	_____

FACTOID: Gideon Sundback invented the zipper in 1913.

Use mental math to find each product.

1. 7 × 10 = _____
2. 16 × 10 = _____
3. 10 × 92 = _____
4. 100 × 8 = _____
5. 50 × 50 = _____
6. 7 × 600 = _____
7. 500 × 200 = _____
8. 5 × 900 = _____
9. 70 × 60 = _____
10. 30 × 400 = _____
11. 200 × 300 = _____
12. 400 × 600 = _____
13. 8 × 1,000 = _____
14. 9 × 3,000 = _____
15. 30 × 5,000 = _____

Circle the form of the verb *to be* that correctly completes each sentence.

16. I (be, am) guessing the number of pennies in the jar.
17. What (is, be) your favorite month?
18. The workmen (been, were) repairing the road in front of our house.
19. Carla (was, were) laughing very loudly.
20. (Is, Are) you the team leader?
21. My Uncle Caleb (been, has been, have been) an astronaut for many years.
22. The old house (is being, are being) torn down.
23. We (be, will be) playing in the orchestra on Saturday night.

Write a sentence using each form of the verb *to be*. Make sure that your sentences are different from the ones above.

24. were _____
25. has been _____
26. was being _____
27. are _____

DAY 9

Read the passage. Then, answer the questions.

The Lost Colony

Englishman Sir Walter Raleigh wanted to start a colony in the New World (North America). In 1585, Raleigh sent colonists to what is now North Carolina. The colonists did not want to work and almost starved to death. They were taken back to England. Two years later, a second group of colonists sailed to the same place as the previous colonists. They worked very hard to survive.

Because of a war involving England, Raleigh lost track of the colonists. In 1591, a ship from England arrived to check on the colonists, but the colonists had disappeared! There was no sign of life. All that the sailors found were some empty trunks, rotted maps, and the word CROATAN carved on the door post of the fort. Croatan was an island 100 miles south of the Lost Colony. No one knows whether the colonists were attacked by the Croatan Indians or the colonists went to live on Croatan Island. The Lost Colony has been a great mystery in American history.

28. Where is the Lost Colony? _____

29. How many years did it take Sir Walter Raleigh to send a ship to check on the

    second group of colonists? _____

30. Why do you think this colony was called the Lost Colony? _____

    _____

31. Which of these statements is false?
    A. The first colonists that Sir Walter Raleigh sent to the New World did not want to work and almost starved to death.
    B. Because of a war involving England, Raleigh lost track of the second group of colonists who went to the New World.
    C. When a ship arrived from England to check on the colonists, they found them alive and well and living with the Croatan Indians.

FITNESS FLASH: Do 10 shoulder shrugs.

* See page ii.

Find each product.

1. 826
    × 47

2. 584
    × 29

3. 249
    × 63

4. 973
    × 51

5. 628
    × 274

6. 831
    × 347

7. 609
    × 149

8. 586
    × 781

Write the past-tense form of each irregular verb in parentheses to complete each sentence.

EXAMPLE:

I (wear) _____*wore*_____ an old coat to school.

9. The telephone (ring) _____ 10 times before she answered it.

10. The contractor (build) _____ a new apartment building every year.

11. Aunt Dawn (feed) _____ her cats three times a day.

12. We each (choose) _____ a friend to go with us to Funland.

13. My brother (spend) _____ all of his allowance on ice cream.

14. The top (spin) _____ for five minutes.

15. Our family (run)_____ in a marathon two summers ago.

16. I (awake) _____ when my dog jumped on my bed.

17. They (become) _____ excited when their team scored a point.

18. My uncle (bring) _____me a T-shirt from his trip.

19. My friend (draw) _____ a picture of me.

20. The starfish (grow) _____a new arm.

DAY 10

Combine words from list A and list B to make compound words. Words from either list can be used as the first part of each compound word. Each word should be used one time.

A		B	
ache	blood	bite	board
clip	craft	head	hound
frost	guard	life	neck
loud	mint	pepper	person
sales	ship	point	silver
turtle	view	space	speaker
ground	watch	wreck	wrist
ware		play	

21. _____ 22. _____

23. _____ 24. _____

25. _____ 26. _____

27. _____ 28. _____

29. _____ 30. _____

31. _____ 32. _____

33. _____ 34. _____

35. _____

Accepting Differences

Accepting differences means accepting another person's qualities and personality just as they are. At times, accepting differences might be challenging. It can become easier with practice, especially as you become more self-aware. Read the following situations. On a separate sheet of paper, write the possible outcomes of not accepting differences. Then, write the benefits of accepting differences.

- You have been assigned to work on a class project with a classmate. He and his family recently immigrated to the United States, and you do not know him well. All of your friends are in another group. The teacher has informed you that there will be no changes made to the groups. You must work with this person and create a project to present to the class by the end of the week.

- You are at a friend's house after school. The family insists that you stay for dinner. You agree. You sit down at the table and look at the food being served. You realize that the food looks and smells very different from your typical dinner at home.

CHARACTER CHECK: Write a 30-second commercial promoting honesty. Share it with a family member.

Estimate the amount of time it will take you to complete the 36 multiplication problems. Find each product. Time yourself.

Estimated Time: _____ **Actual Time:** _____ **Difference Between the Two Times:** _____

1. 6 × 7 = _____
2. 8 × 9 = _____
3. 5 × 5 = _____
4. 11 × 5 = _____

5. 12 × 2 = _____
6. 6 × 9 = _____
7. 9 × 0 = _____
8. 9 × 6 = _____

9. 5 × 10 = _____
10. 11 × 10 = _____
11. 9 × 3 = _____
12. 9 × 12 = _____

13. 12 × 3 = _____
14. 10 × 9 = _____
15. 7 × 4 = _____
16. 6 × 8 = _____

17. 7 × 8 = _____
18. 9 × 11 = _____
19. 12 × 4 = _____
20. 7 × 10 = _____

21. 11 × 12 = _____
22. 7 × 3 = _____
23. 9 × 9 = _____
24. 5 × 11 = _____

25. 7 × 5 = _____
26. 12 × 10 = _____
27. 7 × 9 = _____
28. 10 × 10 = _____

29. 11 × 2 = _____
30. 12 × 6 = _____
31. 8 × 5 = _____
32. 6 × 11 = _____

33. 10 × 3 = _____
34. 8 × 8 = _____
35. 10 × 4 = _____
36. 12 × 11 = _____

Write the past-tense form of each irregular verb in parentheses to complete each sentence.

37. The monkey (eat) _____ four bananas.

38. I was so afraid of the dark that I (shake) _____ when the lights went out.

39. Kai (hold) _____ his breath for one minute.

40. My nose (bleed) _____ for five minutes last night.

41. The students (write) _____ essays telling what they did on their field trip.

42. Alexander (ride) _____ his Shetland pony in the parade last summer.

43. Julie's mother (teach) _____ us how to jump double Dutch.

44. My sisters and I (fight) _____ a lot when we were children.

45. The rain (freeze) _____ when it hit the pavement.

DAY 11

Use the proofreading mark ⌒ to correct the errors with compound words. The first one has been done for you.

My Travel Log

Yesterday after⌒noon, I took the train to Eastland. My grand parents picked me up at the station. At first, I did not see them because the side walk out side the building was very crowded and every one was taller than I am. When ever I tried to look around, some one was in the way. There were two cow boys, some foot ball fans, and three ladies with big suit cases. Finally, I found my grand parents. They said that they had looked every where for me. They took me in side the rail road station for lunch. There is a great café near the news paper stand. Usually, what ever Grandpa orders is good. After lunch, Grandpa drove us to their house. It is on a beach down the road from an old light house. No body operates the light house any more. Tomorrow, we will take a tour.

Choose the word or word phrase from the word bank that has almost the same meaning as the underlined word or phrase in each sentence.

cash crops	indigo
indentured servants	proprietor

_____ 46. George Calvert was the first <u>owner</u> of a colony.

_____ 47. Many Southern farmers grew <u>crops to sell for money</u>.

_____ 48. In 1744, Eliza Lucas developed <u>a blue dye made from a plant</u>.

_____ 49. Originally, <u>people who agreed to work five or seven years to pay their passage to America</u> labored on Southern farms.

FACTOID: Because the moon is 400 times closer to Earth than the sun, the moon and the sun appear to be the same size.

Estimate the amount of time it will take you to complete the 24 multiplication problems. Find each product. Time yourself.

Estimated Time: _____ **Actual Time:** _____ **Difference Between the Two Times:** _____

1. 6 × 3 = _____
2. 8 × 2 = _____
3. 9 × 7 = _____
4. 11 × 6 = _____
5. 8 × 7 = _____
6. 11 × 5 = _____
7. 5 × 7 = _____
8. 6 × 10 = _____
9. 11 × 7 = _____
10. 8 × 8 = _____
11. 9 × 11 = _____
12. 12 × 12 = _____
13. 5 × 12 = _____
14. 7 × 6 = _____
15. 8 × 12 = _____
16. 11 × 8 = _____
17. 10 × 6 = _____
18. 7 × 7 = _____
19. 8 × 6 = _____
20. 12 × 6 = _____
21. 9 × 4 = _____
22. 11 × 9 = _____
23. 12 × 3 = _____
24. 8 × 10 = _____

To show the past tense of an irregular verb, change the spelling. In a sentence, the past participle is used with a helping verb.

EXAMPLE: tear   tore   (have, has) torn

Write each irregular verb under the correct heading.

flown	rang	rung	ate	ring	see	sang
seen	sing	gone	go	sung	flew	saw
began	eaten	eat	bitten	bite	swam	fly
swim	swum	begin	went	begun	bit	

25. Present

26. Past

27. Past Participle

DAY 12

Circle the word that is misspelled in each row and spell it correctly on the line. Use a dictionary if you need help.

28.	refund	remodle	decode	preview
29.	deposet	pretend	deflate	pace
30.	mold	respond	giggel	revise
31.	fiction	shelfes	unsafe	equip
32.	transfer	defend	truthful	penlty
33.	prdict	decide	gossip	fragile
34.	beware	precice	porches	capital
35.	leashes	cipher	estamate	climax
36.	month	friendly	wrench	businiss
37.	jiant	rectangle	guest	greet

Invent a new ice-cream flavor. How is it made? What will you call it? Describe your new flavor.

_____

_____

_____

_____

_____

_____

_____

_____

_____

_____

FITNESS FLASH: Practice a V-sit. Stretch five times.

* See page ii.

Estimate the amount of time it will take you to complete the 36 multiplication problems. Find each product. Time yourself.

Estimated Time:_____ **Actual Time:** _____ **Difference Between the Two Times:** _____

1. 5 × 6 = _____ 2. 7 × 7 = _____ 3. 9 × 8 = _____ 4. 12 × 9 = _____

5. 9 × 5 = _____ 6. 10 × 10 = ____ 7. 7 × 6 = _____ 8. 8 × 7 = _____

9. 8 × 4 = _____ 10. 11 × 3 = _____ 11. 10 × 5 = _____ 12. 5 × 8 = _____

13. 8 × 0 = _____ 14. 6 × 5 = _____ 15. 11 × 4 = _____ 16. 0 × 8 = _____

17. 6 × 12 = _____ 18 5 × 3 = _____ 19. 7 × 8 = _____ 20. 8 × 6 = _____

21. 8 × 3 = _____ 22. 9 × 2 = _____ 23. 12 × 12 = ____ 24. 11 × 8 = _____

25. 10 × 2 = _____ 26. 12 × 5 = _____ 27. 9 × 7 = _____ 28. 11 × 12 = _____

29. 6 × 6 = _____ 30. 10 × 0 = _____ 31. 7 × 11 = _____ 32. 10 × 7 = _____

33. 8 × 9 = _____ 34. 9 × 10 = _____ 35. 5 × 4 = _____ 36. 8 × 11 = _____

Write the future-tense form of each verb in parentheses to complete each sentence.

37. A group (build) _____ a huge rocket.

38. Technicians (check) _____ safety issues.

39. Ian and his dad (map) _____ the journey ahead of time.

40. Ian and his friends (board) _____ the rocket.

41. The announcer (count) _____ down to zero.

42. The rocket (launch) _____ into orbit.

43. The crew (view) _____ Earth from space.

44. They (observe) _____ comets and asteroids.

45. Marshall (record) _____ space sounds.

46. Emily (photograph) _____ interesting things.

Earth's History

Dinosaurs lived long ago—approximately 60 million years ago. Today, all that is left of them are their fossils, bones, and footprints. But, what does 60 million years mean to us? Scientists developed a geologic time scale that illustrates the periods in Earth's history. It can help those of us living today gain some perspective about the time involved in the development of life on Earth.

Read the chart. Then, answer the questions.

47. Earth's history is divided into how many major eras? _____

48. What are the names of the eras?

_____

_____

_____

_____

49. In which era did dinosaurs exist?

_____

50. Into how many periods is the Mesozoic era divided? _____

51. What are the Mesozoic periods' names?

_____

_____

_____

52. In which era do you live?

_____

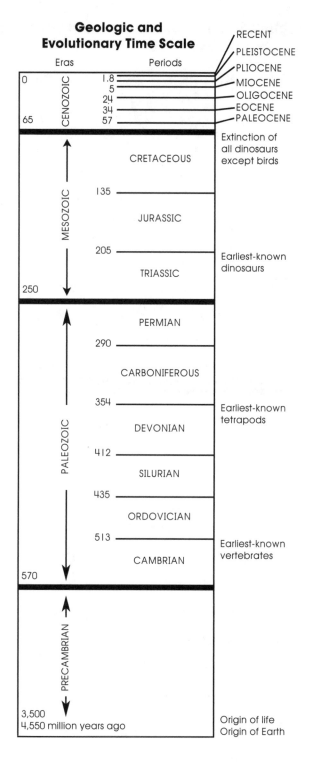

Geologic and Evolutionary Time Scale

Eras	Periods	
		RECENT
CENOZOIC 0	1.8	PLEISTOCENE
	5	PLIOCENE
	24	MIOCENE
	34	OLIGOCENE
65	57	EOCENE / PALEOCENE
MESOZOIC	CRETACEOUS	Extinction of all dinosaurs except birds
	135	
	JURASSIC	
	205	
	TRIASSIC	Earliest-known dinosaurs
250		
PALEOZOIC	PERMIAN	
	290	
	CARBONIFEROUS	
	354	Earliest-known tetrapods
	DEVONIAN	
	412	
	SILURIAN	
	435	
	ORDOVICIAN	
	513	Earliest-known vertebrates
	CAMBRIAN	
570		
PRECAMBRIAN		
3,500		Origin of life
4,550 million years ago		Origin of Earth

FACTOID: Lithium is the lightest metal on Earth.

Eggs are classified primarily by their weight. A dozen small eggs weigh approximately 18 ounces. Medium eggs weigh 21 ounces a dozen. Large eggs weigh 24 ounces a dozen. Extra large eggs weigh a hefty 27 ounces a dozen. Jumbo eggs, which are classified as the largest sellable eggs, weigh 30 ounces a dozen.

Use the information above to answer each question.

1. Six dozen _____ eggs weigh a total of 180 ounces.

2. Which weigh more, 3 dozen jumbo eggs or 6 dozen small eggs? _____

    _____

3. If 5 dozen eggs weigh 120 ounces total, which size are they? _____

4. What is the minimum weight you can have if you have 4 dozen eggs?

    _____ ounces of _____ eggs

5. If you bought a dozen of each size of egg, what would be the total weight

    in ounces? _____

Write the words that make each contraction.

6. shouldn't _____

7. they'll _____

8. I've _____

9. you're _____

10. what's _____

Write the contraction for each pair of words.

11. was not _____

12. he is _____

13. she will _____

14. they would _____

15. you have _____

DAY 14

Correct the journal entry. Cross out each misspelled word and rewrite the word correctly above it.

Febuary 8, 2011

Dear Journel,

It has definately been a busy weekend. My calender was completely full. On Friday morning, I opened the door after the doorbell rang. I was expecting to see my friend and naybor, Adrienne. Instead, I saw Aunt Carol. I was happy and suprised. There was not much time to talk. I had to leave for school in a few minutes, and Mom would head to the library in about an hour. "I took an early train," Aunt Carol explained. "I know everyone will be gone all day. Don't worry about me. I will clean out the cuboards and vacume the living room while your gone. We will catch up tonight. I especialy look forward to the priviledge of talking to you." Then, she gave me a big hug. We talked untill it was time to leave for school.

Write five questions that you would like to ask the leader of your country.

_____

_____

_____

_____

_____

_____

_____

_____

_____

_____

FITNESS FLASH: Touch your toes 10 times.

* See page ii.

A multiple is a number that may be divided by another number without leaving a remainder. List five multiples for each of the following numbers.

EXAMPLE:

2 __**4, 6, 8, 10, and 12**__

1. 5 _____

2. 9 _____

3. 10 _____

4. 12 _____

Common multiples are multiples that two or more numbers share. List three common multiples for each pair of numbers.

EXAMPLE:

4 and 5 __**20, 40, and 60**__

5. 3 and 4 _____

6. 5 and 10 _____

7. 4 and 7 _____

8. 6 and 8 _____

The least common multiple is the smallest multiple that two numbers share. Name the least common multiple for each pair of numbers.

EXAMPLE:

3 and 9 ___**9**___

9. 2 and 9 _____

10. 3 and 4 _____

11. 5 and 6 _____

12. 8 and 10 _____

Adjectives tell *how many*, *what kind*, or *which one* about the nouns they modify. Write an adjective to complete each sentence. At the end of each sentence, write which type of adjective you used. Use each type of adjective at least once.

13. _____ cars got stuck in the traffic jam. _____

14. _____ adventure was amazing. _____

15. The _____ teddy bear cost $25. _____

16. There were _____ camels than lions at the zoo. _____

17. The _____ lizard in the enclosure was huge. _____

DAY 15

Write a synonym for the word in parentheses to complete each sentence. Use a thesaurus if you need help.

EXAMPLE: I had to (finish) _complete_ my work before I could go with my friends.

18. Sarah and Angie go for a (walk) _____ every day except Sunday.

19. It's fun to watch the little colts (play) _____ in the pasture.

20. The electricians have done (enough) _____ work for this week.

21. I cannot (find) _____ the information I need for my report.

22. You should write all of the important events of your (trip) _____ .

23. The lost couple had not had any (food) _____ for two days.

24. Will you please (show) _____ how your new invention works?

25. They will (try) _____ to climb Mount Everest again next summer.

26. The Hubble Space Telescope (completes) _____ one orbit around Earth every 96 minutes.

27. The value of this coin will (grow) _____ over the years.

Animal Stretch

Have you ever watched cats, dogs, or other animals stretch? Yoga is a practice of stretches that improve your body's flexibility and strength. Many common yoga poses are based on the movements of animals, such as dogs, cats, monkeys, and birds. Research your favorite animal. Then, create a stretch that mirrors the way your animal moves. If you need ideas, you may want to research some common yoga poses. Your stretch can be a seated stretch or a standing stretch. Share your move with a friend and see if she can perform your stretch. Can she guess what animal she is copying?

CHARACTER CHECK: Look up the word *responsible* in the dictionary. How are you responsible?

* See page ii.

A negative number is a number that has a value of less than zero. A positive number is a number that is greater than zero. Write the negative numbers on the number line.

1.

_____ _____ _____ _____ _____   0   ⁺1   ⁺2   ⁺3   ⁺4   ⁺5

More than one adjective can be used to modify the same noun. Underline the adjectives in each sentence. Then, circle the words they modify.

2. The wild, eerie wind frightened the children.

3. A fuzzy, brown caterpillar was creeping down the sidewalk.

4. Staci splashed some fresh, cool water on her face.

5. The hot, tired explorers swam in a large, clear lake.

6. The spicy aroma of apple cider filled Jason's small, warm tent.

An adjective that has the suffix *–er* (comparative form) or *–est* (superlative form) is used to compare nouns. Rewrite the adjective in parentheses by adding *–er* or *–est* to complete each sentence.

7. What is the (long) _____ word in the English dictionary?

8. Our back door is (wide) _____ than our front door.

9. Mozart was one of the world's (young) _____ composers.

10. The gorilla is the (large) _____ of all of the apes.

11. New Jersey is a (small) _____ state than Pennsylvania.

DAY 16

Read the passage. Then, answer the questions.

Photosynthesis

Photosynthesis is the process in which plants use sunlight to produce food and oxygen. In addition to light, plants need water and carbon dioxide to grow. A plant gathers water through its roots and takes in carbon dioxide from the air. A compound called chlorophyll helps plants use sunlight. Chlorophyll is what makes plants green.

Plants use energy from the sun to break down the water and carbon dioxide. Through photosynthesis, plants produce oxygen and glucose. Glucose is a type of sugar that plants use for energy. Some people refer to trees as the "lungs of the planet." This is because trees help keep a balance between oxygen and carbon dioxide in the air. When people or animals breathe in oxygen, they exhale carbon dioxide. Plants convert carbon dioxide into oxygen that people and animals can breathe again.

12. What is the main idea of this passage?
    A. People and animals breathe in oxygen.
    B. Plants use energy from the sun.
    C. Photosynthesis is a process through which plants produce food and oxygen.

13. What do plants need to grow?_____

14. What makes plants green?_____

15. What is glucose? _____

16. Why are trees sometimes called the "lungs of the planet"? _____

_____

_____

FACTOID: A camel can drink up to 25 gallons of water in 10 minutes.

Write the integer for each letter on the number line.

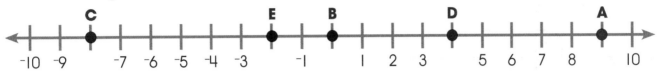

1. A = _____   2. B = _____   3. C = _____   4. D = _____   5. E = _____

Write >, <, or = to compare each pair of numbers.

6. ⁻8 ◯ 8   7. 0 ◯ ⁻3   8. 15 ◯ ⁻16

9. ⁻4 ◯ 4   10. ⁻12 ◯ -20   11. ⁻3 ◯ ⁻4

Write *PA* if the underlined word or group of words is a proper adjective. Write *PN* if the word or group of words is a proper noun.

12. _____ There are many <u>Puerto Rican</u> neighborhoods in New York City.

13. _____ Some people have recently arrived from <u>Puerto Rico</u>.

14. _____ Years ago, many <u>Italian</u> immigrants landed in America.

15. _____ People came from <u>Ireland</u> in the 1800s and 1900s.

16. _____ Some <u>German</u> people immigrated to America too.

17. _____ Some of the first <u>English</u> settlers were the Puritans.

18. _____ They left <u>England</u> for several reasons in the 1600s.

19. _____ <u>Japanese</u> immigrants brought agricultural products such as tea

plants and bamboo roots to the United States.

20. _____ <u>Chinese</u> immigration in the 1850s was fueled by the construction of

_____ the Transcontinental Railroad and the <u>California</u> gold rush.

Choose a word from the word bank that is a synonym for each bold word. Then, write it in the crossword puzzle.

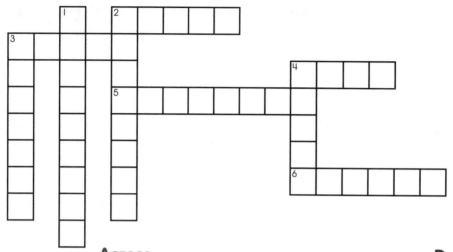

Word bank:
remember
well-known
starving
smart
great
crowd
doctor
grabbed
chew

Across

2. My **intelligent** dog learned a new trick.
3. Your party was **superb**!
4. Jack's puppy likes to **gnaw** on toys.
5. Do you **recall** the phone number?
6. I went to my **physician** when I got sick.

Down

1. On Monday, a **famous** artist will visit us.
2. I was **famished**, so I ate a snack.
3. My aunt **grasped** the railing as she came down the stairs.
4. A **mob** of fans was at the concert.

Below are some sentences about the first president of the United States, George Washington. Read the sentences and put them in the correct chronological order.

_____ When his father died in 1743, Washington went to live on a plantation known as Mount Vernon.

_____ George Washington was born in 1732 in Virginia.

_____ Washington married Martha Dandridge Custis in 1759.

_____ Washington became the first president of the United States in 1789.

_____ George Washington died in 1799.

_____ In 1758, Washington served in the Virginia House of Burgesses.

_____ Washington served in the French and Indian War from 1754–1758.

FITNESS FLASH: Do arm circles for 30 seconds.

* See page ii.

In a fraction, the denominator names the number of equal parts of the whole. The numerator names the number of parts of the whole that are being added. Write a fraction that tells what part of each figure is shaded.

1.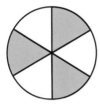

2.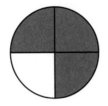

3.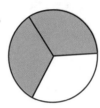

4.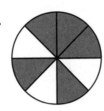

_____

5.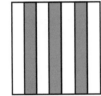

6.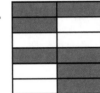

7.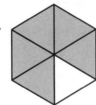

8.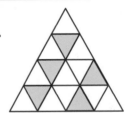

_____

Adverbs are words that modify or describe verbs, adjectives, and other adverbs. Adverbs tell *how, when,* and *where*. Many adverbs end with *-ly*. Write each adverb next to the question it answers.

above	carefully	eagerly	far	hard	here
immediately	inside	lately	quickly	never	often
softly	soon	there	today	upstairs	wildly

9. When?						
10. How?						
11. Where?						

DAY 18

Read each pair of sentences. Circle the word in the first sentence that is the antonym for the bold word in the second sentence.

12. The air was moist and cool after the heavy rain last night.

    Once the sun was out for a couple of hours, the air seemed to be **dry**.

13. A lost dog was enclosed in a pen until the owner came to get her.

    When the dog was **released** to her owner, she jumped up to lick him.

14. Dad was ignorant about the driving laws when he visited England.

    He quickly became **knowledgeable** by reading a book of the rules.

15. Dripping water from our roof will freeze in the winter and make icicles.

    Sometimes, it is spring before the icicles **thaw** and disappear.

16. Madame Proctor purchased a valuable diamond at the auction.

    The diamond turned out to be **worthless** when she discovered that it was fake.

Write a word or group of words from the word bank to complete each sentence.

center of Earth	core	inner core
lithosphere	mantle	outer core

17. The core of Earth has two parts. The _____ is liquid.

    The _____ is solid.

18. One reason that the crust and upper _____

    are brittle is because they are the outermost and coldest layers of Earth.

19. The _____ includes the crust and the uppermost mantle.

20. The _____ is the thickest layer and is extremely hot.

21. As the _____ is approached, pressure and

    temperature increase.

FACTOID: Astronauts clean dishes using wet and dry wipes.

Write each fraction on the number line.

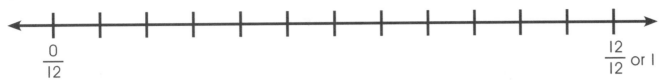

$\frac{0}{12}$

$\frac{12}{12}$ or 1

1. $\frac{3}{12}$ 2. $\frac{7}{12}$ 3. $\frac{10}{12}$ 4. $\frac{1}{12}$ 5. $\frac{5}{12}$

Write >, <, or = to compare each pair of fractions.

6. $\frac{7}{15}$ ◯ $\frac{9}{15}$ 7. $\frac{3}{4}$ ◯ $\frac{6}{8}$ 8. $\frac{4}{6}$ ◯ $\frac{1}{3}$

9. $\frac{5}{9}$ ◯ $\frac{5}{8}$ 10. $\frac{7}{8}$ ◯ $\frac{14}{16}$ 11. $\frac{9}{9}$ ◯ $\frac{8}{8}$

12. $\frac{1}{10}$ ◯ $\frac{1}{5}$ 13. $\frac{14}{20}$ ◯ $\frac{9}{10}$ 14. $\frac{6}{12}$ ◯ $\frac{1}{2}$

Underline the adverb in each sentence. Then, write the verb that the adverb modifies.

15. The cat's broken leg is healing nicely. _____

16. The train moved rapidly down the tracks. _____

17. That chorus sang well. _____

18. Our three bulldogs waited eagerly for their walk. _____

19. The monkeys chattered noisily in the trees. _____

Write an adverb to complete each sentence.

20. The child sat _____ on the stairs.

21. Delicate white snowflakes were falling _____ to the ground.

22. Kirk spoke _____ to his father on the phone.

23. April drove her new car _____ through the middle of town.

24. The old windmill worked _____ after he oiled it.

DAY 19

Read the passage. Then, answer the questions.

Ancient Greece

The people of Ancient Greece lived nearly 4,000 years ago. They created beautiful buildings, and they held the first Olympic Games. The original Olympics were held every four years for more than 1,000 years. The Greeks also came up with the idea of democracy, or government by the people rather than government by a single ruler. The Greeks created small figurines and life-sized statues. They built public buildings, like theaters and stadiums. Modern sports arenas are still based on ancient Greek stadiums.

The Ancient Greeks made many contributions to science, mathematics, and medicine. Greek medical texts were used for hundreds of years. Because Greece is made up of several islands, many Greeks were fishermen and sailors. They established trade routes throughout the ancient world. The Greek poet Homer wrote two epic poems that are still read today. *The Iliad* and *The Odyssey* told the stories of heroes who traveled the world.

25. What is the main idea of this passage?
    A. The ancient Greeks had many accomplishments in art, science, and sports.
    B. The ancient Greeks lived nearly 4,000 years ago.
    C. The ancient Greeks held the first Olympic Games.

26. Name three accomplishments of the ancient Greeks. _____
    _____
    _____

27. What is one way that Greek architecture influenced modern buildings?
    _____
    _____

28. For how many years were the original Olympic Games held? _____

29. How can you tell that the Greeks' accomplishments in medicine were admired?
    _____

FITNESS FLASH: Do 10 shoulder shrugs.

* See page ii.

Write each equivalent fraction.

1. $\dfrac{3}{4} = \dfrac{}{8}$

2. $\dfrac{5}{8} = \dfrac{}{16}$

3. $\dfrac{10}{25} = \dfrac{2}{}$

4. $\dfrac{4}{9} = \dfrac{}{36}$

5. $\dfrac{7}{12} = \dfrac{28}{}$

6. $\dfrac{6}{6} = \dfrac{12}{}$

7. $\dfrac{3}{4} = \dfrac{}{20}$

8. $\dfrac{7}{15} = \dfrac{}{45}$

9. $\dfrac{9}{12} = \dfrac{36}{}$

10. $\dfrac{2}{3} = \dfrac{10}{}$

11. $\dfrac{3}{10} = \dfrac{18}{}$

12. $\dfrac{1}{3} = \dfrac{3}{}$

13. $\dfrac{5}{8} = \dfrac{}{72}$

14. $\dfrac{2}{5} = \dfrac{8}{}$

15. $\dfrac{5}{12} = \dfrac{}{36}$

16. $\dfrac{11}{24} = \dfrac{44}{}$

Write the correct forms of each adverb.

Adverb	Adverb That Compares Two Actions	Adverb That Compares More Than Two Actions
EXAMPLE:		
loudly	*more loudly*	*most loudly*
17. quietly		
18. smoothly		
19. frequently		
20. clearly		
21. closely		
22. patiently		
23. soon		
24. roughly		
25. neatly		
26. fast		

DAY 20

Read each pair of sentences. Circle the word in the first sentence that is the antonym for the bold word in the second sentence.

27. Ben enjoys Saturdays because he goes to his grandparents' farm.

    He **dislikes** when it is time to leave them and their farm animals.

28. Hurricanes and tornadoes can destroy anything in their paths.

    Sometimes, it takes months to **repair** the damage they cause.

29. When Nancy is at the park, she often plays on the swings.

    She **seldom** has to wait to take her turn.

30. It was foolish of Ricky not to study for the science test.

    When he saw his grade, he wished that he had been more **sensible** and had studied for it.

31. When Cathy woke, she had to face reality.

    She realized that her dreams the night before were just **fantasy**.

A sentence should clearly indicate the noun for which a pronoun stands. Revise the underlined words to make the meaning of each sentence clear.

EXAMPLE:

When the tree hit the telephone pole, it burst into flames.

When the tree hit the telephone pole, the tree burst into flames.

32. When the president said goodbye to the senator, he looked confident.

    _____

33. Marty told Ben that his scrape would heal if he put antiseptic on it.

    _____

34. Before the key could fit the keyhole, it had to be made smaller.

    _____

CHARACTER CHECK: During the day, watch for people who are demonstrating kindness. At the end of the day, share with a family member the kindness you observed.

Growing Crystals

Have you ever looked closely at ice crystals? What about salt crystals? In this activity, you can grow all kinds of crystals yourself!

Materials
- 10 tsp. water
- 5 tsp. salt
- 5 tsp. laundry bluing
- 1 tsp. ammonia
- food coloring
- charcoal briquettes
- pie pan
- teaspoon
- bowl

Procedure
1. With an adult, mix the water, salt, laundry bluing, and ammonia in a bowl.
2. Place the charcoal pieces in the pie pan. Pour just enough of this solution over the charcoal so that it covers the bottom of the pan.
3. To make colorful crystals, drizzle the food coloring over the top of the pile of charcoal. Or, to make white crystals with a blue tint, do not use any food coloring.
4. Crystals will begin to form right away on the charcoal and in the pan. As the solution evaporates, add more to the pan. Caution: If you pour the solution directly on the charcoal, the crystals, which are very fragile, will be crushed. Even blowing very hard on the crystals will knock them over.

What's This All About?
Charcoal is a porous material. It absorbs the liquid in the bottom of the pie pan, and the liquid that is poured over it evaporates, leaving a crystal garden. The garden will continue to grow until the pan runs out of the solution or until the crystals grow too tall to support their own weight and fall.

Air Pressure

How does the carbon dioxide in Earth's atmosphere affect the air temperature?

Materials
- 2 aquarium thermometers
- ruler
- tape
- 2 clear plastic storage containers with lids
- water
- 2 effervescent antacid and pain reliever tablets
- 2 identical lamps with 200-watt bulbs

Procedure
1. Place the aquarium thermometers approximately 1 inch (2.5 cm) below the opening of the plastic storage containers so that they can be read from the outside. Tape the thermometers in place.
2. Add water to each plastic storage container to a depth of approximately 1.5 inches (3.8 cm). Place the lid on each container.
3. Lift the lid on one container slightly and quickly drop in two effervescent antacid and pain reliever tablets. The tablets will react with the water to produce carbon dioxide gas. Close the lid quickly to trap the carbon dioxide gas within the "atmosphere" of the container. Label the container.
4. Place one lamp above each container. The distance and location of the lamp above each container should be identical.
5. Take a temperature reading every 10 minutes until three consecutive readings are the same for each container. Record your readings in a graph.

What's This All About?
Burning fossil fuels to obtain energy creates chemical by-products that are dangerous in the atmosphere. Carbon dioxide, a greenhouse gas, is one chemical by-product that concerns some scientists. They think that the increase of carbon dioxide in the atmosphere is affecting the planet's temperatures. The carbon dioxide in the atmosphere absorbs solar energy and traps excess heat. Within this century, carbon dioxide levels have risen, as have global temperatures.

There are two opposing views concerning global warming: one is that the warming is part of Earth's natural cycle, and the other is that human activities are increasing global temperatures.

The 50 States

Label as many U.S. states as you can. Use an atlas to finish if you need help.

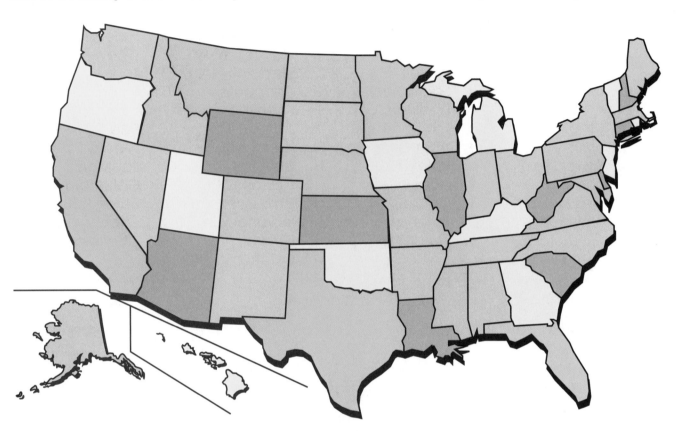

Alabama (AL)	Alaska (AK)	Arizona (AZ)	Arkansas (AR)
California (CA)	Colorado (CO)	Connecticut (CT)	Delaware (DE)
Florida (FL)	Georgia (GA)	Hawaii (HI)	Idaho (ID)
Illinois (IL)	Indiana (IN)	Iowa (IA)	Kansas (KS)
Kentucky (KY)	Louisiana (LA)	Maine (ME)	Maryland (MD)
Massachusetts (MA)	Michigan (MI)	Minnesota (MN)	Mississippi (MS)
Missouri (MO)	Montana (MT)	Nebraska (NE)	Nevada (NV)
New Hampshire (NH)	New Jersey (NJ)	New Mexico (NM)	New York (NY)
North Carolina (NC)	North Dakota (ND)	Ohio (OH)	Oklahoma (OK)
Oregon (OR)	Pennsylvania (PA)	Rhode Island (RI)	South Carolina (SC)
South Dakota (SD)	Tennessee (TN)	Texas (TX)	Utah (UT)
Vermont (VT)	Virginia (VA)	Washington (WA)	West Virginia (WV)
Wisconsin (WI)	Wyoming (WY)		

BONUS

U.S. States and Capitals

Match each U.S. state with the correct capital.

a. Montpelier ?	n. Salem ?	A. Salt Lake City	N. Helena
b. Honolulu	o. Boston	B. Lansing Mich	O. Cheyenne
c. Hartford	p. Pierre ND	C. Bismarck SD.	P. Topeka
d. Lincoln	q. Sacramento	D. Annapolis -	Q. Richmond
e. Columbus	r. Frankfort	E. Nashville	R. Trenton
f. Madison	s. Montgomery	F. Juneau	S. Boise
g. St. Paul	t. Augusta	G. Harrisburg	T. Albany
h. Springfield	u. Raleigh	H. Dover	U. Jackson
i. Phoenix	v. Austin	I. Carson City	V. Columbia
j. Des Moines	w. Concord ? NJ.	J. Little Rock	W. Baton Rouge
k. Providence	x. Tallahassee	K. Indianapolis	X. Atlanta
l. Olympia	y. Jefferson City	L. Denver	Y. Charleston
m. Santa Fe		M. Oklahoma City	

1. ____ Alabama
2. ____ Alaska
3. ____ Arizona
4. ____ Arkansas
5. ____ California
6. ____ Colorado
7. ____ Connecticut
8. ____ Delaware
9. ____ Florida
10. ____ Georgia
11. ____ Hawaii
12. ____ Idaho
13. ____ Illinois
14. ____ Indiana
15. ____ Iowa
16. ____ Kansas
17. ____ Kentucky
18. ____ Louisiana
19. ____ Maine
20. ____ Maryland
21. ____ Massachusetts
22. ____ Michigan
23. ____ Minnesota
24. ____ Mississippi
25. ____ Missouri
26. ____ Montana
27. ____ Nebraska
28. ____ Nevada
29. ____ New Hampshire
30. ____ New Jersey
31. ____ New Mexico
32. ____ New York
33. ____ North Carolina
34. ____ North Dakota
35. ____ Ohio
36. ____ Oklahoma
37. ____ Oregon
38. ____ Pennsylvania
39. ____ Rhode Island
40. ____ South Carolina
41. ____ South Dakota
42. ____ Tennessee
43. ____ Texas
44. ____ Utah
45. ____ Vermont
46. ____ Virginia
47. ____ Washington
48. ____ West Virginia
49. ____ Wisconsin
50. ____ Wyoming

Where I Live

Draw the shape of your state or province and label where you live. Draw your state or province's flower and bird.

BONUS

Take It Outside!

Summer is the perfect time to plan a family day trip to your state or province's capital. With an adult, discuss some of the places that you would like to visit. Talk with friends and neighbors who have visited the capital and get their recommendations. Make a list of the places you decide you would like to see in your state or province's capital. Check online to gather information about guided tours of these places, their hours of operation, and their admission prices. Write a proposal and present it to your family, encouraging them to place this day trip on the family's summer calendar.

With an adult, take a bike ride or nature walk around your neighborhood. Your goal is to look for samples of compound words. Be sure to bring a pen and a notebook. Every now and then, stop at a safe spot, record some of what you have seen, and list the compound words that you have discovered, such as *ladybug, firefly*, and *sunflower*. When you return home, write a poem or short story using at least two of the compound words that you discovered on your outdoor excursion.

Summer is an especially good time for a cookout. Schedule a cookout and invite your family, friends, and neighbors to attend. Plan a menu that includes a choice of items for an adult to grill, such as chicken, hamburgers, and veggie burgers. Poll your neighbors before the cookout. The poll will help you determine the amount of food to purchase. Prior to the barbecue, make a bar graph to display near the grill, enabling people to see the neighborhood preferences.

* See page ii.

Monthly Goals

Think of three goals to set for yourself this month. For example, you may want to read for 30 minutes each day. Write your goals on the lines. Post them someplace visible, where you will see them every day.

Draw a line through each goal as you meet it. Feel proud that you have met your goal, and set new ones to continue to challenge yourself.

1. _____

2. _____

3. _____

Word List

The following words are used in this section. Use a dictionary to look up each word that you do not know. Then, write three sentences. Use a word from the word list in each sentence.

align	manor
elaborate	monotonous
epicenter	raze
inscription	tier
lunge	varnish

1. _____

_____

2. _____

_____

3. _____

_____

_____

Introduction to Strength

This section includes fitness and character development activities that focus on strength. These activities are designed to get you moving and thinking about strengthening your body and your character.

Physical Strength

Like flexibility, strength is important for a healthy body. Many people think that a strong person is someone who can lift an enormous amount of weight. However, strength is more than the ability to pick up heavy barbells. Having strength is important for many everyday activities, such as helping with yardwork or helping a younger sibling get into a car. Muscular strength also helps reduce stress on your joints as your body ages.

Everyday activities and many fun exercises provide opportunities for you to build strength. Carrying bags of groceries, riding a bicycle, and swimming are all excellent ways to strengthen your muscles. Classic exercises, such as push-ups and chin-ups, are also fantastic strength-builders.

Set realistic, achievable goals to improve your strength based on the activities that you enjoy. Evaluate your progress during the summer months and set new strength goals for yourself as you accomplish your previous goals.

Strength of Character

As you build your physical strength, work on your inner strength as well. Having a strong character means standing up for your beliefs, even if others do not agree with your viewpoint. Inner strength can be shown in many ways. For example, you can show inner strength by being honest, standing up for someone who needs your help, and putting your best effort into every task. It is not always easy to show inner strength. Think of a time when you showed inner strength, such as telling the truth when you broke your mother's favorite vase. How did you use your inner strength to handle that situation?

Use the summer months to develop a strong sense of self, both physically and emotionally. Celebrate your successes and look for ways to become even stronger. Reflect upon your accomplishments during the summer, and you will see positive growth on the inside and on the outside.

Simplify each fraction.

1. $\dfrac{56}{6}$ = _____

2. $\dfrac{14}{4}$ = _____

3. $\dfrac{38}{8}$ = _____

4. $\dfrac{52}{8}$ = _____

5. $\dfrac{18}{4}$ = _____

6. $\dfrac{35}{5}$ = _____

7. $\dfrac{14}{6}$ = _____

8. $\dfrac{10}{8}$ = _____

Find the fraction of each number.

9. $\dfrac{2}{5}$ of 10 = _____

10. $\dfrac{1}{4}$ of 32 = _____

11. $\dfrac{4}{6}$ of 24 = _____

12. $\dfrac{3}{5}$ of 60 = _____

Direct objects are nouns or pronouns that complete or receive the action of the verb. They follow only action verbs. Circle the verb and underline the direct object in each sentence.

EXAMPLE:

John Smith (guided) the colonists in the New World.

13. The banker put the money in the vault.

14. Alejandro bought some groceries at the supermarket.

15. The crowd begged the musicians to play more.

16. We found some rare coins in an old glass jar.

17. The sun melted the icicles on the house.

18. My brother, the quarterback, made a touchdown.

19. The movers loaded the furniture into the truck.

20. Trenton sold 50 tickets for the raffle drawing.

21. The tangled string ruined my kite.

DAY 1

Write a synonym for each word.

22. jump _____

23. crawl _____

24. quickly _____

25. tired _____

26. sprint _____

Write an antonym for each word.

27. narrow _____

28. near _____

29. horrible _____

30. open _____

31. find _____

Read the passage. Then, answer the questions.

Earth is like a huge magnet. It has a magnetic field. Its magnetism is the strongest at the north and south poles. When a rock forms, magnetic particles within the rock align themselves with Earth's magnetic field. They will point toward either the north or south pole. There are some rocks that do not point to the current north and south poles. Scientists conclude that either the north and south poles have moved, or the rocks themselves have moved since they first formed. Most scientists think that the rocks and continents have moved. Geologists use this information to determine how the continents have moved over time.

32. Why is Earth compared to a magnet? _____

33. Where are Earth's strongest points of magnetism? _____

34. How can geologists study the movements of the continents? _____

_____

FACTOID: There are 750,000 known kinds of insects.

To multiply fractions, first multiply the numerators. Then, multiply the denominators. When you multiply two fractions, the product is smaller than the two factors. Find each product. Simplify each fraction. Then, draw a fraction picture to illustrate each answer.

1. $\dfrac{1}{2} \times \dfrac{3}{4} = $ _____

2. $\dfrac{1}{4} \times \dfrac{1}{2} = $ _____

3. $\dfrac{1}{2} \times \dfrac{1}{3} = $ _____

4. $\dfrac{1}{3} \times \dfrac{2}{3} = $ _____

5. $\dfrac{2}{3} \times \dfrac{1}{6} = $ _____

6. $\dfrac{1}{3} \times \dfrac{1}{4} = $ _____

7. $\dfrac{2}{3} \times \dfrac{4}{5} = $ _____

8. $\dfrac{2}{3} \times \dfrac{2}{3} = $ _____

9. $\dfrac{1}{4} \times \dfrac{2}{3} = $ _____

10. $\dfrac{3}{4} \times \dfrac{2}{5} = $ _____

The direct object of a verb receives the action of the verb. The indirect object of a verb comes before the direct object and usually tells to whom or for whom the action is done. Underline each verb once. Underline each direct object twice. Then, circle each indirect object.

11. Jose gave the wiggling puppy a bath.

12. Peter wished his grandmother a happy birthday.

13. Jamal gave Alan the tire swing.

14. The waiter handed Kent his burger platter.

15. Quinn, the girl who sits in the back, offered Tommy her pencil.

16. Aunt May knitted Davetta a yellow scarf.

17. Mr. Slider gave the cat a treat.

18. The first graders wrote their pen pals letters.

19. The new neighbor made our family stir-fry.

20. Roberta saved Rico some sweet corn.

DAY 2

Read the passage. Then, answer the questions.

The Mayan Empire

The Maya lived in Central America from about 2600 BC to about AD 900. The Mayan Empire covered present-day Guatemala, Belize, and El Salvador, as well as part of Honduras and southeastern Mexico. The Maya built elaborate stone temples, palaces, and buildings called observatories from which they could watch the movements of the planets and stars. They created a calendar with 260 days to mark special days in their civilization. Every 20th day, the Maya held a festival.

The Mayan ruins in Chichèn Itzá, Mexico, include performance stages, markets, and even a ball court. Many Mayan foods are still eaten in Central America, including maize (corn), beans, chili peppers, and squash. The Maya wore beautiful woven fabrics, feathered headdresses, and hats. No one is sure why the Maya disappeared, but archaeologists hope to find out.

21. What is the main idea of this passage?
    A. The Maya built many great buildings.
    B. The Maya suddenly disappeared.
    C. The Maya lived in Central America thousands of years ago.

22. How long did the Maya live in Central America? _____
    _____

23. Which modern countries did the Mayan Empire cover? _____
    _____

24. What do people do at an observatory? _____
    _____

25. What was special about the Mayan calendar? _____
    _____
    _____

FITNESS FLASH: Do 10 lunges.

* See page ii.

Find each product. Simplify each fraction.

1. $\dfrac{1}{2} \times \dfrac{3}{5} =$ _____

2. $\dfrac{2}{3} \times \dfrac{2}{3} =$ _____

3. $\dfrac{3}{4} \times \dfrac{1}{4} =$ _____

4. $\dfrac{2}{3} \times \dfrac{5}{7} =$ _____

5. $\dfrac{4}{5} \times \dfrac{2}{7} =$ _____

6. $\dfrac{1}{2} \times \dfrac{1}{6} \times \dfrac{2}{3} =$ _____

7. $\dfrac{2}{3} \times \dfrac{5}{6} \times \dfrac{1}{4} =$ _____

8. $\dfrac{1}{3} \times \dfrac{5}{7} \times \dfrac{3}{5} =$ _____

9. $\dfrac{2}{3} \times \dfrac{3}{4} \times \dfrac{1}{2} =$ _____

10. $\dfrac{8}{9} \times \dfrac{1}{3} \times \dfrac{3}{4} =$ _____

Replace each underlined word with a preposition from the word bank to show a different relationship between the words in each sentence.

behind	near	through	under	until

EXAMPLE: Grayson found his backpack ~~under~~ _____*near*_____ his desk.

11. Julie stood <u>beside</u> _____ me at the parade.

12. Did you leave this box <u>on</u> _____ the bench?

13. The children will play <u>after</u> _____ dark.

14. The bats flew <u>into</u> _____ the window.

The object of the preposition is the noun or pronoun following a preposition. Write an object (noun or pronoun) for each underlined preposition.

15. That boy had a glass <u>of</u> _____ .

16. We climbed <u>over</u> a _____ .

17. Jayla fell <u>off</u> her _____ .

18. Far <u>below</u> the _____ , we could see the river.

DAY 3

Write the homophone in parentheses that matches each definition. Use a dictionary if you need help.

19. _____ : grinds or crushes with the teeth (chews, choose)

20. _____ : inexpensive; of little value (cheap, cheep)

21. _____ : a large mammal with long shaggy fur (bare, bear)

22. _____ : having little or no color; not bright (pail, pale)

23. _____ : a house on a large estate (manner, manor)

24. _____ : a series of rows, one above another (tears, tiers)

25. _____ : a long, slender object usually shaped like a cylinder (pole, poll)

26. _____ : something to be learned (lessen, lesson)

Use the time line to answer each question about the events leading up to the Revolutionary War.

1754	1763	1765	1770	1773	1774	1775
French and Indian War	King George III limits Western settlement.	Stamp Act	Boston Massacre	Boston Tea Party	Intolerable Acts	Battles fought at Lexington and Concord

27. How many years after the French and Indian War did the Boston Massacre occur? _____

28. Which events occurred in Boston? _____

_____

29. Which occurred first—the Stamp Act or the Intolerable Acts? How many years were between these events? _____

30. Who gave a proclamation to limit Western settlement? _____

31. Where were the battles fought in 1775? _____

FACTOID: There are 88 keys on a standard piano.

Match each term with its definition.

1. _____ fraction

A   the answer you get when you divide one number by another number

2. _____ improper fraction

B.   the number found below the line in a fraction

3. _____ quotient

C.   a number that names a part of a set or whole

4. _____ mixed number

D.   the number found above the line in a fraction

5. _____ denominator

E.   a number that has a whole number and a fraction

6. _____ numerator

F.   a fraction whose numerator is greater than or equal to its denominator

Fill in each blank and answer each question.

7.   Write $2 \div 9$ as a fraction. _____

8.   Write $15 \div 7$ as an improper fraction.

_____

9. $82 \div 7$ can be written _____ or $7\overline{)82}$.

What is the divisor? _____

What is the remainder? _____

Write it as a mixed number. _____

10. What kind of fractions are $\frac{28}{5}$, $\frac{17}{12}$, and $\frac{59}{7}$? _____

Write a mixed number for each fraction. _____

A prepositional phrase is made up of a preposition and its object. Underline each prepositional phrase.

EXAMPLE: <u>around the playground</u>

11. between the bases

12. along the trail

13. until four o'clock

14. near the window

15. the circus elephant

16. the math problem

17. a hanging light

18. outside the door

19. are the bridges

20. the wet streets

21. under the house

22. in the barn

23. things that have gills

24. your guide

25. how you will be

DAY 4

Circle the correct homophone(s) to complete each sentence.

26. Tanya (new, knew) how to get along with (new, knew) people.

27. The (our, hour) hand on (our, hour) new clock does not move correctly.

28. I like to (read, reed) magazines about sports.

29. You can (buy, by) a good used TV in the store next (to, two, too) the shopping mall.

30. Spencer and Jack invited me to come to (there, their) house after school.

31. Mrs. Brinks told her students to bring (to, two, too) pencils to class for the test.

32. I (see, sea) a beautiful sunset down by the (see, sea) every night.

33. Our cat, Cosby, sometimes chases his (tale, tail).

Strength in Numbers!

Find a pair of dice and get ready to become stronger! Study the list of activities below. Roll the dice and add the numbers shown. Then, choose one of the activities and do the same number of repetitions as the sum from the dice. For example, if you rolled a seven, you might choose to do seven jumping jacks. Write the number of repetitions beside each exercise. You must complete each exercise once, and no exercise can be repeated during a round. Repeat rounds of exercises to match your fitness level.

Exercise	Repetitions	Repetitions	Repetitions	Repetitions	Repetitions
push-ups					
sit-ups					
jumping jacks					
arm circles					
hopping on one leg					
lunges					
leg lifts					

FITNESS FLASH: Do 10 squats.

* See page ii.

To divide fractions, multiply the first fraction by the reciprocal of the divisor. Find each quotient. Simplify each fraction.

EXAMPLE: $\dfrac{2}{3} \div \dfrac{4}{5}$

$$\dfrac{2}{3} \times \dfrac{5}{4} = \dfrac{10}{12} = \dfrac{5}{6}$$

1. $\dfrac{5}{8} \div \dfrac{2}{6} =$ _____

2. $\dfrac{3}{4} \div \dfrac{1}{2} =$ _____

3. $\dfrac{1}{5} \div \dfrac{3}{10} =$ _____

4. $\dfrac{1}{6} \div \dfrac{1}{12} =$ _____

5. $\dfrac{4}{5} \div \dfrac{2}{3} =$ _____

6. $\dfrac{2}{8} \div \dfrac{3}{4} =$ _____

7. $\dfrac{6}{7} \div \dfrac{8}{12} =$ _____

8. $\dfrac{1}{5} \div \dfrac{1}{2} =$ _____

9. $\dfrac{9}{12} \div \dfrac{8}{10} =$ _____

10. $\dfrac{3}{4} \div \dfrac{1}{7} =$ _____

11. $\dfrac{7}{9} \div \dfrac{2}{6} =$ _____

12. $\dfrac{4}{9} \div \dfrac{2}{5} =$ _____

Write *and*, *or*, or *but* to complete each sentence.

13. Jenna _____ Lamont are on the same baseball team.

14. She wanted the team color to be blue, _____ he preferred red.

15. The players chose their favorite positions, _____ they were very pleased.

16. Jenna plays either first base _____ in the outfield.

17. In the first inning, Jenna hit a single _____ Lamont hit a double.

18. Their team was winning, _____ the other team caught up in the fourth inning.

19. Jenna stopped one runner, _____ Lamont let the other runner get to third base.

20. Their team scored three more runs, _____ the score was tied.

Read the passage. Then, answer the questions.

Harriet Tubman

Harriet Tubman used the Underground Railroad, a secret system of safe houses and people, to escape from slavery. Tubman went to Philadelphia, Pennsylvania, where she could live as a free person. Escaping from slavery was hard and dangerous. But, Tubman was brave, and once she was free, she wanted to help others become free too. She returned to the South and helped her family members and other slaves escape. Harriet Tubman worked on the Underground Railroad from 1850 to 1860.

When the Civil War started, Tubman became a spy. Many women worked as spies during the war, but few took as many risks as Tubman did. Tubman knew the land in the South, and she knew ways to travel without being caught. She gathered information to help the Northern army. Tubman even led a group of African American soldiers on a raid. The group freed more than 700 slaves. No woman had led American soldiers on a raid before. Tubman also worked as a nurse. She cared for wounded African American soldiers and slaves. After the war, Tubman helped the freed slaves. She opened her home to take care of the elderly, and she worked for women's rights. Harriet Tubman was one of the strongest and bravest women in American history.

21. What is the main idea of this passage?
    A. Harriet Tubman was a strong woman.
    B. Harriet Tubman was a slave who escaped.
    C. Harriet Tubman was a strong woman who spent her life helping others.

22. Number the events in the order they happened.

    _____ Tubman worked for women's rights.

    _____ Tubman escaped to freedom in the North.

    _____ Tubman worked as a spy.

    _____ Tubman's work helping slaves escape ended when the war started.

23. What did Tubman do during the war that no other woman had ever done?

    _____

24. Name something Tubman did after the war. _____

> **CHARACTER CHECK:** Draw a comic strip showing a character who demonstrates loyalty.

When adding or subtracting decimals, first line up the decimals. If the amount of decimal places in the numbers is not the same, add zeros to the end of the number with fewer decimal places. Solve each problem.

EXAMPLE: 3.45 + 5.923 = **3.450**
$$\begin{array}{r} 3.450 \\ +\ 5.923 \\ \hline 9.373 \end{array}$$

1. 18.91 + 11.5 = _____

2. 34.09 − 9.407 = _____

3. 3.806 + 5.29 = _____

4. 185.04 − 165.9 = _____

5. 437.7 + 13.906 = _____

6. 379.76 − 37.435 = _____

7. 42.881 + 8.96 = _____

8. $224.00 − $116.98 = _____

Write an interjection from the word bank on each line. Use an exclamation point to show strong emotion. Use a comma to show weak emotion.

| Great | Hey | Oh | Oh no | Phew | Wow | Yes |

9. _____ why is the classroom so busy today?

10. _____ I forgot that we are pretending to build a pyramid.

11. _____ It looks like ancient Egypt!

12. _____ We tried to decorate in an ancient style.

13. _____ Millie remembered to wear her costume.

14. _____ I almost forgot to bring mine!

15. _____ I remembered that it was in my backpack!

DAY 6

Write homophones from the word bank to complete each sentence.

I	bee	I'll	clothes	buy	know	ate	sent
eye	Aunt	Isle	blew	by	band	eight	
be	ant	close	blue	No	banned	cent	

EXAMPLE: _____*I*_____ think that _____*I*_____ have something in my ___*eye*___ .

16. Chris will _____ stung by that bumble_____ if he gets any closer.

17. My _____ Lola saw an _____ hill on the sidewalk.

18. The _____ was _____ from playing at the concert.

19. _____ visit the _____ of Man in June.

20. Please _____ the door to the _____ closet.

21. Pat _____ me one _____ for good luck.

22. My _____ jeans _____ away in the wind.

23. We went _____ the mall to _____ some cards.

24. My brother _____ _____ pancakes for breakfast.

25. _____ , I do not _____ how to play a musical instrument.

You have just learned that you will share a bedroom with a younger brother or sister. Write a letter explaining to your family why you feel that this is or is not a good idea.

_____

_____

_____

_____

_____

_____

FACTOID: Approximately one million Earths could fit inside the sun.

Fill in the table with information from the passage and answer the question.

Amanda opened a checking account on May 15 with $500.25. On May 31, she deposited $496.80. On June 4, she withdrew $145.00 to buy a bicycle. On June 15, she deposited $435.20. On June 30, she deposited $600.00. On July 1, she withdrew $463.00 to buy a sleeping bag and pay for camp. On July 15, she deposited $110.00. On July 24, she withdrew $600.00 to buy a computer.

Date	Deposit	Withdrawal	Total $
May 15	$500.25		$500.25
May 31			
June 4			
June 15			
June 30			
July 1			
July 15			
July 24			

1.   How much money did Amanda have in her account on July 25? _____

A sentence fragment is a phrase that does not express a complete thought. A complete sentence is a phrase that expresses a complete thought. A complete sentence tells whom or what the sentence is about and what happened to the person or thing. Draw lines to match sentence fragments to make complete sentences.

2.   Folklore is passed   on your head?

3.   The early cattle ranchers   escaped from his cage.

4.   Nassim rides his   drove their cattle to the market.

5.   The snake in the science corner   from generation to generation.

6.   Can you balance a book   bike to school most days.

Write *F* if the phrase is a sentence fragment or *S* if it is a complete sentence.

7.   _____ All of my friends like spaghetti.

8.   _____ Went camping last summer.

9.   _____ Answered the most questions.

10.   _____ Mr. Able turned on the lights.

DAY 7

An analogy shows a relationship between two sets of words or phrases. Complete each analogy.

EXAMPLE: *Preview* is to *previewed* as *decide* is to _____ *decided*

11. *Hear* is to *ear* as *talk* is to _____.

12. *Griddle* is to *pancake* as *pot* is to _____.

13. *Author* is to *book* as *artist* is to _____.

14. *Business* is to *businesses* as *address* is to _____.

15. *Research* is to *researcher* as *garden* is to _____.

16. *Breakfast* is to *lunch* as *morning* is to _____.

17. *Control* is to *controllable* as *reason* is to _____.

18. *TV* is to *commercial* as *magazine* is to _____.

19. *Manager* is to *store* as *principal* is to _____.

Use the letters from each spelling word to make new words. Try to make four- and five-letter words. Use each letter from the spelling word only once in each new word.

EXAMPLE: journeys *yours*   *runs*   *sore*   *nose*

20. enemies _____ _____ _____ _____

21. vocabulary _____ _____ _____ _____

22. inscription _____ _____ _____ _____

23. purpose _____ _____ _____ _____

24. suspended _____ _____ _____ _____

25. examiner _____ _____ _____ _____

26. pendulum _____ _____ _____ _____

27. luxurious _____ _____ _____ _____

28. monotonous _____ _____ _____ _____

FITNESS FLASH: Do five push-ups.

* See page ii.

Find each product. Add extra zeros when necessary.

1.   41.5
      × 0.17

2.   1.09
      × 0.68

3.   3.05
      × 85.2

4.   0.003
      ×   3.9

5.   7.4
      × 0.07

6.   0.09
      × 2.3

7.   0.035
      × 0.02

8.   0.005
      ×   55

Write _S_ if the sentence is a complete sentence, _F_ if it is a fragment, or _R_ if it is a run-on sentence.

9. _____ Orangutans are rare animals.

10. _____ Live in rain forests in Borneo and Sumatra.

11. _____ They belong to the ape family, along with chimpanzees and gorillas, and they are larger than most chimpanzees and smaller than most gorillas.

12. _____ About three to five feet (about 91 to 152 cm) tall.

13. _____ Their arms are extremely long.

14. _____ Male orangutans can weigh as much as humans.

15. _____ Female orangutans are half the size of males.

16. _____ Orangutans live in nests in trees, and they swing from branch to branch, and they do not walk on the ground often.

Read the passage. Then, answer the questions.

Biologists

Biologists are scientists who study life on Earth. Another name for *biology* is *life science*. Biologists study plants, animals, and even bacteria. They study organisms that live in the air, in the water, in the soil, and even in the human body. Some biologists observe large animals that live in the desert or jungle, and others look at tiny life forms through microscopes. Biologists also study how ecosystems function. An ecosystem is a community in which plants and animals live together. It can be as large as Earth itself or as small as a single cell. All parts of an ecosystem work together to sustain the creatures living there. A change in even one part of an ecosystem can affect all other parts. Biologists use the information that they learn about life on Earth to understand how to protect animals and plants and how people's actions affect their own ecosystem.

17. What is the main idea of this passage?

    A. Biologists study the different life forms on Earth.

    B. Ecosystems can be large or small.

    C. Some biologists use microscopes in the laboratory.

18. What is another name for *biology*? _____

19. What are some things that biologists study? _____

_____

20. What is an ecosystem? _____

_____

21. What might happen if one part of an ecosystem is changed? _____

_____

22. Would you like to be a biologist? Why or why not? _____

_____

FACTOID: There are approximately 50 million penguins in Antarctica.

Find each product.

1.	0.12 × 6	2.	0.08 × 7	3.	4.6 × 3	4.	5.05 × 8	5.	6.5 × 13

6.	1.906 × 28	7.	7.0216 × 52	8.	6.65 × 77	9.	5.364 × 93	10.	27.035 × 93

Write *D* if the sentence is declarative, *In* if it is interrogative, *E* if it is exclamatory, or *Im* if it is imperative. Then, add the correct ending punctuation to each sentence.

11. _____ Mountains rise where Earth's surface is under pressure

12. _____ Are mountains still forming on Earth

13. _____ Yes, and some of the old ones are wearing down

14. _____ Tell me how that happens

15. _____ Do the wind and rain wear them down

16. _____ Yes, but it takes millions of years for that to happen

17. _____ Is that why the Appalachians are more rounded than the Rockies

18. _____ Yes, the Appalachian Mountains are about 150 million years older than the Rocky Mountains

19. _____ Wow! That makes them 250 million years old

20. _____ What is the highest mountain in the United States

21. _____ Oh my! Mount McKinley is 20,320 feet (6,193.5 m) tall

22. _____ Estimate Mt. McKinley's height in miles

DAY 9

Complete each analogy.

EXAMPLE:

Tree is to lumber as wheat is to _____ *flour* _____ .

23. Bricks are to wall as fingers are to _____ .

24. Pages are to book as _____ are to the United States.

25. Finger is to hand as toe is to _____ .

26. Brake is to stop as gas pedal is to _____ .

27. Apple is to tree as grape is to _____ .

28. Foal is to horse as puppy is to _____ .

29. Space is to rocket as _____ is to car.

30. Bird is to nest as lion is to _____ .

31. Playwright is to play as sculptor is to _____ .

Integrity Interviews

Having integrity means showing moral principles, such as honesty. Talk with several family members and neighbors. Ask them to tell you about someone they know who has integrity. Encourage the people with whom you talk to provide examples of how they see the person demonstrating integrity in her life. After completing the interviews, write a 60-second commercial promoting integrity as a way of living. Be sure to include a catchy slogan as well as a jingle. After your commercial is complete, record it and share it with family, friends, and neighbors.

FITNESS FLASH: Do 10 sit-ups.

* See page ii.

Find each quotient.

1. $3\overline{)5.4}$ 2. $4\overline{)10.4}$ 3. $7\overline{)25.9}$ 4. $6\overline{)27.6}$ 5. $0.2\overline{)17.8}$

6. $3.4\overline{)80.24}$ 7. $2.5\overline{)114.75}$ 8. $1.9\overline{)149.15}$ 9. $3.8\overline{)262.58}$ 10. $6.1\overline{)338.55}$

Write a subject to complete each sentence.

11. _____ fascinated Megan.

12. _____ need water.

13. _____ collapsed suddenly.

14. _____ misplaced his new watch.

15. _____ know how to operate the computers.

Write a predicate to complete each sentence.

16. The package _____ .

17. A team of horses _____ .

18. The famous actor _____ .

19. Sarah and Taneshia _____ .

20. Anthills _____ .

DAY 10

A simile is a figure of speech in which two unlike things are compared using *like* or *as*. Write the actual meaning of each simile.

21. Her voice lilted like soft music. _____

22. The cat's fur is as smooth as silk. _____

23. The water is like a sparkling sapphire. _____

24. Kristen soaked up the information like a sponge. _____

25. He stood as straight as an arrow. _____

26. Write your own simile or metaphor. _____

_____

Write words from the word bank to complete the paragraph.

Seismologists	fault	earthquake	above	epicenter
Seismic waves	focus	energy	beneath	fracture

An _____ is the sudden shaking of the ground that

happens when _____ stored in rock is released. A

_____ is a break, or _____,

in the earth's crust. As rock breaks, stored energy moves along the fault. The

hypocenter, or _____, is where an earthquake begins.

The point on the earth's crust that is directly _____ the

focus is called the _____ . An earthquake begins

_____ the earth's surface. _____, or

shock waves, move out from the focus and cause the ground to shake.

_____ study and record these shock waves and determine

the size of the earthquake.

CHARACTER CHECK: Share with an
adult five things for which you are grateful.

Solve each problem.

1.
```
  24.98
  14.20
  10.19
+ 82.29
```

2.
```
  89.82
  42.47
   8.18
+ 75.03
```

3.
```
  86,945
   6,913
   7,428
+  5,317
```

4.
```
  3,921
  1,823
  4,765
+ 5,283
```

5.
```
   674
× 392
```

6.
```
  5,978
×   703
```

7. $72\overline{)95,634}$

8. $82\overline{)809,791}$

Solve each problem. Simplify if possible.

9. $6\dfrac{3}{5} \times 1\dfrac{2}{8} =$ _____

10. $2\dfrac{1}{2} \times 4\dfrac{1}{5} =$ _____

11. $2\dfrac{2}{5} + 6\dfrac{3}{4} =$ _____

12. $8 - 2\dfrac{3}{4} =$ _____

Underline each simple subject once. Underline each simple predicate twice.

13. A brown owl watches from the tall tree.

14. Worms burrow in the soft dirt.

15. A large orca surfaces on the horizon.

16. Moths flutter at the streetlight.

17. An elephant trumpets loudly in the distance.

18. The spider on the web captures an unaware fly.

19. The gazelles stampede across the plains.

20. Koalas climb to the top of gum trees to eat eucalyptus leaves.

21. The soaring hawk scans the land for small rodents.

22. A red fox slinks through the underbrush.

DAY 11

Read the passage. Then, answer the questions.

Elections

Many leaders in the United States and Canada are elected to office. In an election, people vote for candidates whom they want to serve in particular roles in the government. They may also vote for or against issues, such as funding a new park or changing a law. Most elections have secret ballots. In this type of election, no one can see how you vote. Without a secret ballot, people may try to influence the way others vote. For many years, election booths used a system in which voters pulled levers to select their candidates. Many modern voting machines use punch cards or computers to record people's votes. It is important for people to vote so that they have a say in which leaders are running their city, state, or country. Some people consider the right to vote to be the most important right of a citizen.

23. What is the main idea of this passage?
    A. Many leaders are elected to office.
    B. In an election, people vote for leaders and to change laws.
    C. Voting is an important right for citizens.

24. What types of issues might people cast votes for? _____
    _____

25. What does it mean to have a secret ballot? _____
    _____

26. How did people cast votes in the past?_____
    _____

27. How do many people cast votes today? _____
    _____

FACTOID: Two stars that orbit each other are called *doubles.* Half of the stars in the universe are doubles.

Complete each fact family.

EXAMPLE:

$78 \times 42 = \mathbf{3{,}276}$

$42 \times 78 = \mathbf{3{,}276}$

$3{,}276 \div 42 = \mathbf{78}$

$3{,}276 \div 78 = \mathbf{42}$

1. $39 \times 56 = 2{,}184$

   _____

   _____

   _____

2. $95 \times 37 = 3{,}515$

   _____

   _____

   _____

3. $49 \times 76 = 3{,}724$

   _____

   _____

   _____

4. $151 \times 27 = 4{,}077$

   _____

   _____

   _____

5. $3{,}762 \div 38 = 99$

   _____

   _____

   _____

6. $26{,}320 \div 47 = 560$

   _____

   _____

   _____

7. $48{,}306 \div 83 = 582$

   _____

   _____

   _____

8. $194 \times 92 = 17{,}848$

   _____

   _____

   _____

Underline each complete subject. Circle each simple subject.

9. A giant tortoise may live 100 years.

10. Baby pandas are pink and have no fur at birth.

11. An alligator's eye has three eyelids.

12. Giraffes have the same number of neck bones as humans.

Underline each complete predicate. Circle each simple predicate.

13. The squirrel lives in a nest high in an old elm tree.

14. He awakens in his leafy nest late in the morning.

15. The squirrel's family left early in the morning.

16. He races along the elm's branches.

17. The squirrel scampers down the tree trunk.

DAY 12

Write a word from the word bank to complete each simile.

| flat | midnight | mouse | rocket | shiny | swings |

18. The theater was as dark as _____ before the movie started.

19. Jayla was as quiet as a _____ as she studied for the test.

20. My dad's new shoes are as _____ as a new penny.

21. The deflated ball is as _____ as a pancake.

22. Taylor's brother _____ like a monkey on the jungle gym.

23. The first batter's baseball flew like a _____ out of the ballpark.

You have been given the task of adding one month to the year. What would you call your month? When in the year would it occur? What would people celebrate during the month? Write a paragraph describing your new month.

_____

_____

_____

_____

_____

_____

_____

_____

_____

_____

_____

FITNESS FLASH: Do 10 lunges.

*See page ii.

Answer each question.

1. What time was it 2 hours and 30 minutes earlier?_____

2. What time was it 1 hour and 15 minutes earlier? _____

3. What time will it be in 4 hours and 30 minutes? _____

4. What time was it 3 hours and 45 minutes earlier?_____

5. Kevin got to school at 8:25 A.M. He was 15 minutes late. What time did school start? _____

6. Stacy has 45 minutes left before the concert ends. It is 10:05 P.M. What time will the concert end? _____

Underline each complete subject once and circle each simple subject. Underline each complete predicate twice and draw a line through each simple predicate.

7. Carmen walks carefully along the rocky shore.

8. Pools of water collect in rocky crevices near the shore.

9. Tide pools are home to sea plants and animals.

10. Seaweed is the most common tide pool plant.

11. They provide food and shelter for a variety of animals.

12. Carmen sees spiny sea urchins attached to a rock.

13. Their mouths are on their undersides.

14. Their sharp teeth cut seaweed into little pieces.

DAY 13

A metaphor is a comparison of two different things without using *like* or *as*. A metaphor is an example of figurative language, or language that paints a picture in the reader's mind. Write your own metaphors.

EXAMPLE:

People are *mirrors; you can see yourself in them* .

15. Sleep is _____ .

16. Happiness is _____ .

17. Life is _____ .

18. Friendship is _____ .

19. Anger is _____ .

Armloads of Strength!

Collect empty water or soft drink bottles of different sizes and fill each bottle halfway with water, sand, or pebbles. Use your bottles for arm curls to improve your strength.

Hold a bottle by your side. Standing with your feet shoulder-width apart, turn your hand so that your palm is faceup. Pull your hand slowly toward your chest and inhale deeply. As you exhale, lower your hand by your side. Do 8–10 repetitions and switch arms. As you become stronger, fill your bottle with increasing amounts of water, sand, or pebbles. With a marker, draw a line for each increment to track your progress.

FACTOID: Walruses can walk on all four fins as fast as a person can run.

* See page ii.

Write the next number in each number pattern.

1. 4, 8, 16, 32, 64, _____

2. 1, 4, 7, 6, 9, 12, 11, _____

3. 1, 4, 7, 10, 13, 16, _____

4. 3, 3, 6, 5, 5, 10, 8, 8, 16, 13, 13, _____

5. 3, 5, 8, 12, 17, 23, _____

6. 6, 11, 16, 21, _____

7. 6, 36, 66, 96, _____

8. 1, 5, 9, 8, 12, 16, 15, 19, 23, 22, _____

If the sentence has a compound subject, write *CS* and circle the two simple subjects. If the sentence has a compound predicate, write *CP* and circle the two simple predicates. Write *N* if the sentence has neither a compound subject nor a compound predicate.

9. _____ People have planted crops and raised animals for about 10,000 years.

10. _____ The ancient Chinese and Japanese practiced freshwater and saltwater farming.

11. _____ The Japanese raised oysters as early as 2000 BC.

12. _____ Fish and shellfish have long been sources of protein for Southeast Asian people.

13. _____ Overfishing and pollution led to the decline of ocean animals over the years.

14. _____ Sea farming and ranching help restore the food supply.

15. _____ Mariculturists, or sea farmers, raise and sell lobsters and shrimp.

16. _____ Oysters grown on farms often grow larger and taste better than wild oysters.

DAY 14

Read the passage. Then, answer the questions.

The Trail of Tears

People of different cultures lived in North America before European explorers arrived. As Europeans began to settle in the New World, they competed with American Indians for land and other resources, such as gold. Over time, the New World was divided into states, and a government was formed. The U.S. government passed laws in the 1830s making it legal to force American Indians to relocate if settlers wanted their land. The Cherokee and other American Indian groups had to move from the southeastern United States to lands farther west. Thousands of American Indians traveled more than 1,000 miles (1,600 kilometers) on foot from their homelands to the land that later became the U.S. state of Oklahoma. Many people died from disease or hunger along the route. The name *Trail of Tears* was given to this event in U.S. history because of the struggles people faced on their journeys. Today, the descendants of the survivors of the Trail of Tears make up the Cherokee Nation.

17. What is the main idea of this passage?

    A.   Many people from Europe settled in the New World.

    B.   Some American Indians still live in Oklahoma.

    C.   The Trail of Tears was the forced relocation of American Indians in the United States.

18. What did European settlers compete with American Indians for? _____

_____

19. How did the U.S. laws that were passed in the 1830s affect American Indians?

_____

_____

20. Where were American Indians forced to move? _____

_____

21. What is the Trail of Tears? _____

_____

FITNESS FLASH: Do 10 squats.

* See page ii.

Solve each problem. Follow the order of operations.

1. (6 x 2) + 8 = _____

2. (10 + 10) ÷ 2 = _____

3. 3 + (8 x 2) = _____

4. 6 x (3 + 3) = _____

5. 14 ÷ 2 + 3 = _____

6. 10 x 10 ÷ 25 = _____

7. 21 ÷ 7 x 2 = _____

8. (17 − 7) ÷ 5 = _____

9. (5 x 2) + 3 = _____

10. 50 ÷ 5 + 3 = _____

A predicate noun is a noun that follows a linking verb and tells something about the subject. Underline each linking verb. Circle each predicate noun. Then, draw an arrow from each predicate noun to the subject it tells about.

11. The zebra mussel is a bivalve originally found in Europe.

12. That girl in the third row is my sister.

13. Mrs. Stamey is a fifth-grade teacher.

14. I am a good student.

15. A solar calculator is a great math tool.

16. Jupiter is a massive ball of gas.

17. Venus is the second planet from the sun.

18. The first-chair trombone player is Marcus Bolan.

19. Our sun is actually a star.

20. That lumpy, dark green yarn will be an afghan someday.

DAY 15

Circle the two words that are being compared in each sentence. Then, write _S_ if the comparison is a simile. Write _M_ if it is a metaphor.

21. _____ The trees are like soldiers standing at attention.

22. _____ When I looked down from the airplane, the cars on the highway were as small as ants.

23. _____ The sound of waves lapping on the shore reminded me of dogs taking a long drink.

24. _____ Twenty circus clowns were like sardines packed in one car.

25. _____ The fans' stamping feet in the bleachers were beating drums.

Most earthquakes occur at plate boundaries. An epicenter is the place on Earth's surface above an earthquake's focus. Study the map of epicenters and answer the questions.

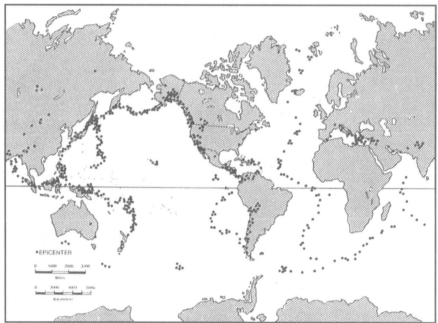

26. Draw a line around the areas with the most earthquake activity.

27. Why do most earthquakes occur at plate boundaries? _____

_____

CHARACTER CHECK: What does it mean to be optimistic?

Write the missing part of each equation.

1. $67 \times \underline{\hspace{2cm}} = 603$

2. $\underline{\hspace{2cm}} \times 77 = 385$

3. $2,210 \div \underline{\hspace{2cm}} = 85$

4. $5,518 \div \underline{\hspace{2cm}} = 62$

5. $19,347 - \underline{\hspace{2cm}} = 18,470$

6. $23,432 + \underline{\hspace{2cm}} = 24,089$

7. $32 \times \underline{\hspace{2cm}} = 6,400$

8. $56,993 - \underline{\hspace{2cm}} = 55,598$

9. $\underline{\hspace{2cm}} + 34,561 = 40,090$

10. $50,000 \div \underline{\hspace{2cm}} = 1,250$

11. $19,263 + \underline{\hspace{2cm}} = 66,390$

12. $\underline{\hspace{2cm}} - 80,399 = 110,099$

A predicate adjective is an adjective that follows a linking verb and tells something about the subject. Underline each linking verb. Circle each predicate adjective. Then, draw an arrow from each predicate adjective to the subject it tells more about.

13. Ants in the house are disgusting.

14. Juicy hamburgers on the grill are delicious.

15. That backyard deck was unvarnished.

16. Jenna's batting abilities are great.

17. The cake that she decorated is beautiful.

18. The dent from the baseball was sizeable.

19. Terrance will feel better after he takes his medicine.

20. Luke's back was sore from shoveling sand into the sandbox.

21. Mrs. Tribble was ecstatic when she saw that her son had cut the grass.

22. Wendy and I were happy with our performance on the tennis court.

DAY 16

Write *S* if the sentence contains a simile. Write *M* if it contains a metaphor.

23. _____ The fruit salad is a rainbow of colors.

24. _____ The pineapple slices are as yellow as the sun.

25. _____ The strawberries are little rubies.

26. _____ The grapes are light green globes.

27. _____ The marshmallows look like tiny white clouds.

Read this part of the U.S. Declaration of Independence. Then, answer the questions.

We hold these truths to be self-evident, that all men are created equal, that they are endowed by their Creator with certain unalienable Rights, that among these are Life, Liberty, and the pursuit of Happiness. —That to secure these rights, Governments are instituted among Men, deriving their just powers from the consent of the governed, —That whenever any Form of Government becomes destructive of these ends, it is the Right of the People to alter or to abolish it, and to institute new Government, laying its foundation on such principles and organizing its powers in such form, as to them shall seem most likely to effect their Safety and Happiness.

28. What are the basic rights of all people according to the Declaration

   of Independence? _____

29. Why are governments "instituted," or created? _____

30. What should people do if they feel the government is not acting in their

   best interest?_____

   _____

FACTOID: The Arctic permafrost can be more than 1,400 feet (426.7 m) deep.

Write the missing numbers in each list. Then, write the rule.

1.

M	N
15	20
40	45
90	___
35	___

Rule: **M + 5 = N**

2.

M	N
25	36
19	30
57	___
___	84

Rule: **M + 11 = N**

3.

M	N
54	45
89	80
73	___
___	61

Rule: **M –** _____

4.

M	N
48	37
12	1
___	19
24	___

Rule: _____

5.

M	N
8	48
4	24
10	___
6	___

Rule: _____

6.

M	N
21	7
30	10
18	___
12	___

Rule: _____

7.

M	N
7	63
___	81
___	54
3	27

Rule: _____

8.

M	N
10	120
___	144
9	108
___	132

Rule: _____

Underline the complete verb and circle the helping verb in each sentence.

EXAMPLE: Jack (was) working in town.

9. Jasmine is walking to the park with her friends.

10. My mother has shopped at that department store for many years.

11. I might have called if I had known you were home.

12. The airport is closed because of yesterday's snowstorm.

13. Jim does enjoy sports.

14. Mark is playing outdoors with Sam.

15. Dana does finish her homework every day.

16. Misty and Courtney are watching TV.

DAY 17

Read the passage. Then, answer the questions.

The United Nations

The United Nations (UN) is a group of countries that work to promote world peace and good relationships between countries. The UN was formed in 1945, after World War II ended. People from 50 countries went to San Francisco, California, to discuss ways to encourage international cooperation. The UN's Security Council has 15 countries, of which five are permanent members (China, France, the Russian Federation, the United Kingdom, and the United States.) These five countries can block proposals brought to the council by voting against them. The other countries on the council are elected to two-year terms. The UN is led by a secretary-general who serves a five-year term. The UN provides peacekeepers to countries at war, helps victims of natural disasters such as flooding, promotes workers' rights, and provides food, medicine, and safe drinking water to those in need. The organization tries to help all people, regardless of where they live.

17. What is the main idea of this passage?

    A. The United Nations helps victims of natural disasters.

    B. The United Nations works to promote peace around the world.

    C. The United Nations was formed in 1945.

18. After what world event was the United Nations formed?_____

_____

19. What can the five permanent members of the Security Council do?

_____

20. How long does the secretary-general serve?_____

21. What are three ways that the United Nations helps people around the world?

_____

_____

_____

FITNESS FLASH: Do five push-ups.

* See page ii.

Match each geometric term with its definition.

1. _____ segment	A.	lines that never meet
2. _____ ray	B.	rays with the same endpoint
3. _____ angle	C.	the distance around a circle
4. _____ perpendicular lines	D.	the unit used when angles are measured
5. _____ parallel lines	E.	lines that intersect to form a right angle
6. _____ diameter	F.	has an endpoint or starting point and can go from there in only one direction
7. _____ radius	G.	a part of a line that can be named by its endpoints
8. _____ circumference	H.	a line connecting the center of a circle to any point on the edge of the circle
9. _____ degree	I.	a segment that passes through the center of a circle and has both endpoints on the circle

Combine each pair of sentences to write a compound sentence using *and* or *but*.

10. The frogs sleep during the day.
    They hunt for food at night.

    _____

    _____

11. A parrot's bright colors are easy to see in a tree.
    A tree boa's green color makes it difficult to spot.

    _____

    _____

12. A fruit bat has a long nose.
    It has large eyes to help it see in the dark.

    _____

    _____

DAY 18

An idiom is a phrase that states one thing but means another. Draw a line to match each idiom with its meaning.

EXAMPLE: It was <u>raining cats and dogs</u>. (The sentence means that it was raining hard.)

13. I can do math problems standing on my head.

14. Who let the cat out of the bag?

15. Charlie is a chip off the old block.

16. Jenna will sleep like a log.

17. Cora and Alexis are like two peas in a pod.

Who told the secret?

She will sleep very well tonight.

I know math well.

The two friends are very similar.

He is just like his father.

Write _T_ for true or _F_ for false for each statement.

18. _____ A volcano is an opening in the crust of the earth through which lava, gases, ash, and rocks erupt.

19. _____ Volcanic material can build up to form mountains.

20. _____ These mountains can form only on land.

21. _____ All magma comes from Earth's core.

22. _____ Most volcanoes happen underwater.

23. _____ Mid-ocean ridges form when magma rises to fill a gap between diverging tectonic plates.

24. _____ Most volcanoes on land occur at diverging plate boundaries.

25. _____ Volcanoes on land occur on the edges of continents or on islands.

26. _____ When two plates converge, compression forces rocks upward to make mountains.

FACTOID: Iceland is a nation built on volcanoes.

Draw a picture to illustrate each geometric term.

1. segment	2. parallel lines	3. circumference
4. ray	5. congruent	6. radius
7. angle	8. diameter	9. perpendicular lines

Draw three lines under the letter that needs to be capitalized in each sentence.

10. "automobiles emit poisonous gases," continued Helen's teacher.

11. Helen said, "i think that power plants and oil refineries must cause pollution too."

12. "yes, they emit a lot of sulfur dioxide and nitrogen oxide."

13. Mr. Hill said, "erupting volcanoes spew sulfur dioxide into the atmosphere."

14. "weather conditions affect how far pollutants travel," said Mr. Hill.

15. "britain's acid rain can fall in Scandinavian countries."

16. Mr. Hill said, "trees in those countries are being harmed by acid rain."

DAY 19

Choose the correct meaning of the bold idiom in each sentence.

17. He is a **big cheese** at his school.
    - A. cafeteria worker
    - B. principal
    - C. very important person

18. My dad is the **top dog** at his job.
    - A. loudest one
    - B. parts supplier
    - C. one in charge; boss

19. After working all afternoon in the yard, Dad and I decided to **call it a day** and go to dinner.
    - A. stop
    - B. talk
    - C. rake leaves

20. She did not talk about her family because she did not want to reveal **the skeletons in her closet**.
    - A. her family secrets
    - B. where she kept trash
    - C. the end of a scary story

21. Tommy would **give you the shirt off his back** if necessary.
    - A. lend you a shirt
    - B. help any way he could
    - C. keep you warm

22. Maria had the answer to Connor's question **on the tip of her tongue**.
    - A. unable to think of the answer
    - B. could not talk
    - C. close to being remembered

If you could live in one time period in history, which period would you choose? Why? What do you think your life would be like on a daily basis? (What would you wear? What would you eat? What would you do for fun?) Write a paragraph about your life in that time period.

_____

_____

_____

_____

_____

_____

FITNESS FLASH: Do 10 sit-ups.

* See page ii.

To find the perimeter of a figure, add the lengths of its sides. Find the perimeter of each figure.

1. 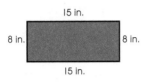 _____ inches	2. 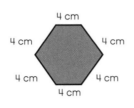 _____ centimeters	3. 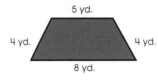 _____ yards
4. 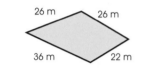 _____ meters	5. 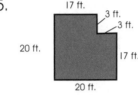 _____ feet	6. 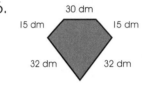 _____ decimeters

Write the name of each person correctly.

7. cousin sylvia _____

8. uncle vernon _____

9. jerry andrews _____

10. aunt martha _____

11. paulo joe rollo _____

12. grandfather murray _____

13. mr. and mrs. foster _____

14. dr. c. l. smith _____

15. ms. maxine marshall _____

16. miss tiffany tyler _____

Read the passage. Then, answer the questions.

Meteorologists

Most people have seen weather forecasters on TV. People who study the weather are called meteorologists. Most of their jobs are performed off camera in offices or laboratories where they study the weather. Meteorologists study past weather patterns to help them predict future weather. They take readings of temperature, wind speed, atmospheric pressure, and precipitation (rain or snow) to forecast the weather. They may use satellites, airplanes, and weather balloons to collect additional data. Meteorologists develop computer models to predict how climate and weather might change in the future. They also study how weather phenomena, such as tornadoes, form. An important part of a meteorologist's job is giving people accurate information in case of an emergency. If your community is being threatened by a storm, such as a hurricane, you need to know when it might strike and how to stay safe.

17. What is the main idea of this passage?
    A. Weather forecasters often appear on TV.
    B. Tornadoes and hurricanes can cause great damage.
    C. Meteorologists study the weather.

18. Why do meteorologists study weather patterns of the past? _____
   _____

19. What does a meteorologist consider when forecasting the weather? _____
   _____

   _____

20. How can computer models help? _____

   _____

21. What might a meteorologist tell you about a hurricane? _____

   _____

CHARACTER CHECK: Make a list of at least five ways that you can show respect at home and at school. Share the list with a family member.

Paper Airplane

The paper airplane you will create in this activity demonstrates the movement of an airplane in response to the air through which it is traveling. If you work on your design carefully, you can get your airplane to soar like an eagle!

A.

Materials
- sheet of paper (8 ½" x 11")
- scissors
- tape

B.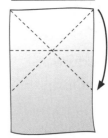

Procedure

1. Fold the upper edge of the paper to the opposite side of the paper. (A) Unfold and repeat with the other side. You should now have an X on your page. Fold the top to the bottom of the X created by the first two folds. (B)

C.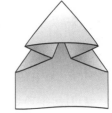

2. Fold in the middle crease on both sides, bringing the top corners toward the bottom of the X. Now, the paper should look like a house. (C)

3. Fold the tip of the roof to the gutter. (D)

D.

4. Fold the airplane in half so that the folds are not showing. (E)

5. Fold down the wings. The body of the airplane should be no more than a half inch (1.27 cm) tall. (F)

E.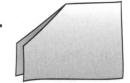

6. Fold the outer quarter inch (0.635 cm) of the airplane wing. Tape the two wings together at the middle fold. (G)

7. Cut two small flaps in the back of the wings in the sections illustrated. These will help direct the movement of the airplane. (G)

F.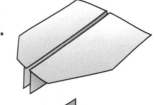

8. By bending the flaps on the back of the wing, you can get the airplane to bank either left or right. If you bend both flaps the same way, you can get the airplane to climb sharply into the atmosphere.

G.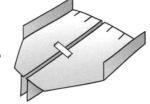

BONUS

Human Nerves

People are able to feel because we have nerves. Some places in our bodies have more nerves than others. Complete this activity to see which places have more nerves and are more sensitive.

Materials
- partner
- paper clip

Procedure
1. Open the paper clip so that the two endpoints are pointing in the same direction, at least one inch (2.54 cm) apart.
2. Ask a partner to place his arm on a table and to close his eyes. You will touch the paper clip's endpoints to different parts of his fingers and arm to see if he can tell whether you are using one end of the paper clip or two.
3. Begin by touching his fingertips with two endpoints. Ask him if he feels one or two points. Tell him whether he is correct or incorrect. Repeat with several different fingers, changing from one to two points and back again.
4. Slowly test your partner's nerves by touching the points to his mid-fingers, palms, wrists, and both sides of the forearm. Change from one to two points at random.

What's This All About?

Nerves, which detect when a body part is touched, are distributed all over the human body. However, nerves are not distributed evenly. By finding out where your partner can feel both ends of the paper clip, you also find out where the body's nerves are closest together. What do you notice about the function of the body parts that seem to have a lot of nerves?

The Mayflower Compact

Read the passage. Then, circle *fact* or *opinion* for each statement.

The Pilgrims were a group of people who disagreed with how the Church of England was run. They wanted to go to a place where they could establish their own church. They received permission to travel to Virginia, where they could worship as they pleased. In September of 1620, about 50 Pilgrims and about 50 other Englishmen (whom the Pilgrims called "Strangers") set sail for America on a ship called the *Mayflower*. In November of 1620, the ship arrived at Cape Cod in present-day Massachusetts. The water to the south was too rough and dangerous, so they decided to settle where they were.

Because the trip had not turned out as planned, some of the Strangers talked about leaving the group. But, the group believed that they had a better chance for survival if they all stuck together, and they had a better chance of sticking together if they agreed at the start to follow certain rules. So, they wrote an agreement called the Mayflower Compact. Many people consider the Mayflower Compact to be the first form of self-government in America's history. The document declared that the group would stay together and form their own laws and government. All who signed promised to follow these laws. Forty-one men signed the compact. (Women did not sign because the did not have many rights at that time.) They elected John Carver as their first governor and set out to look for freshwater. After exploring the area, the travelers decided to settle nearby in Plymouth.

1. The Pilgrims' ideas about the church were better than England's ideas.   fact opinion

2. The *Mayflower* sailed in 1620.   fact opinion

3. Signing the Mayflower Compact was a good idea.   fact opinion

4. Forty-one men signed the Mayflower Compact.   fact opinion

5. John Carver was the smartest person on the *Mayflower*.   fact opinion

6. About 100 people traveled to America on the *Mayflower*.   fact opinion

7. The *Mayflower* did not land where the Pilgrims had planned.   fact opinion

8. The Mayflower Compact was a perfect agreement.   fact opinion

BONUS

The Branches of the U.S. Government

Write the name of the U.S. branch of government (legislative, executive, or judicial) for each responsibility.

1. can impeach the president _____

2. writes bills _____

3. approves or vetoes bills _____

4. interprets and examines laws _____

5. appoints justices _____

The U.S. government is divided into three branches. Each branch is given different but equal powers. Write the responsibilities of each branch in the pie chart.

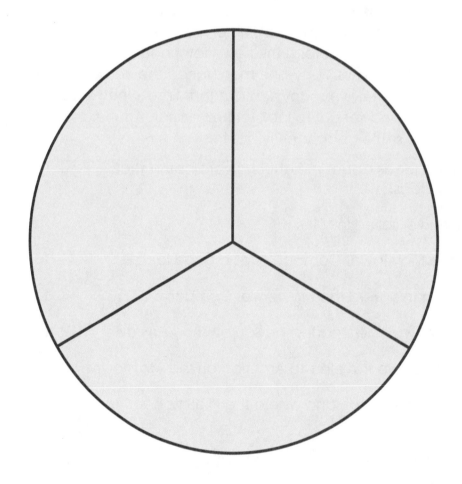

Reading Rainfall Maps

Precipitation maps, or rainfall maps, use patterns to show areas with varying amounts of rainfall or snow. Compare the precipitation maps of Arizona and the main island of Hawaii.

Annual Rainfall

Hawaii

Arizona

Map Key

less than 25 inches

25 to 200 inches

more than 200 inches

Kamuela

Honokaa

Hilo

Kailua-Kona

Map Key

less than 8 inches

8 to 16 inches

more than 16 inches

Flagstaff

Phoenix

Yuma

Tucson

1. Which state receives more rainfall? _____

2. How much annual rainfall does Hilo, Hawaii, receive? _____

3. What does [ ] on the Arizona map represent? _____

4. What does [ ] on the Hawaii map represent? _____

5. Which city is in the driest area in Hawaii? _____

6. Which city on the Arizona map receives the most rainfall? _____

7. Which two cities in Arizona receive 8 to 16 inches (20.32 to 40.64 cm) of

    rain annually? _____ and _____

8. Which two cities in Hawaii receive 25 to 200 inches (63.5 to 508 cm) of

    rain annually? _____ and _____

BONUS

Take It Outside!

Invite family members to go with you to an outdoor market. Be sure to bring a pen and a notebook. Once at the market, begin your hunt for decimals. As you travel the aisles, look at prices. When you locate a decimal, write down the decimal's location and how it is used. On your return home, have some fun with your decimal discoveries. Make a poster informing others of the various "hiding" places decimals have at the market.

Weekends in the summer provide a wonderful opportunity for your family to get together with neighbors for some fun. Invite your family and neighbors to join you for an afternoon paper airplane competition. Provide people with paper to make their airplanes. Have a tape measure available to measure the flight distances. Ask people to take turns flying their paper airplanes. After each throw, measure the distance and list the distance on a chart. After everyone has flown her paper airplane, check the chart and announce the winner of the paper airplane neighborhood competition.

With a family member, go for a walk in a local park. Bring a pencil and a notebook. As you explore the park, keep track of what is in the park and where park attractions are located. Once you are familiar with the park, find a place to sit with your family member and make a map. Be sure to include a compass rose with direction arrows and a key for symbols used on the map. Then, share your map with friends to assist them in finding their way around the park.

Monthly Goals

Think of three goals to set for yourself this month. For example, you may want to learn five new vocabulary words each week. Write your goals on the lines. Post them someplace visible, where you will see them every day.

Draw a line through each goal as you meet it. Feel proud that you have met your goals and set new ones to continue to challenge yourself.

1. _____

2. _____

3. _____

Word List

The following words are used in this section. Use a dictionary to look up each word that you do not know. Then, write three sentences. Use a word from the word list in each sentence.

depicted	industrial
gazing	ornately
gigantic	propel
hazardous	revolution
immigrant	sapling

1. _____

_____

2. _____

_____

3. _____

_____

Introduction to Endurance

This section includes fitness and character development activities that focus on endurance. These activities are designed to get you moving and thinking about developing your physical and mental stamina.

Physical Endurance

What do climbing stairs, jogging, and riding your bike have in common? They are all great ways to build endurance!

Having endurance means performing an activity for a period of time before your body becomes tired. Improving your endurance requires regular aerobic exercise, which causes your heart to beat faster. You also breathe harder. As a result of regular aerobic activity, your heart becomes stronger and your blood cells deliver oxygen to your body more efficiently.

Summer provides numerous opportunities to improve your endurance. Although there are times when a relaxing activity is valuable, it is important to take advantage of the warm mornings and sunny days to go outside. Choose activities that you enjoy. Invite a family member to go on a walk or a bicycle ride. Play a game of basketball with friends. Leave the relaxing activities for when it is dark, too hot, or raining.

Set an endurance goal this summer. For example, you might jog every day until you can run one mile without stopping. Set new goals when you meet your old ones. Be proud of your endurance success!

Mental Endurance

Endurance applies to the mind as well as to the body. Showing mental endurance means sticking with something. You can show mental endurance every day. Staying with a task when you might want to quit and continuing until it is finished are ways that you can show mental endurance.

Build your mental endurance this summer. Maybe you want to earn some extra money for a new bike by helping your neighbors with yard work. But, after one week of working in your neighbors' yards, you discover that it is not as easy as you thought that it would be. Think about some key points, such as how you have wanted that new bike for months. Be positive. Remind yourself that you have been working for only one week and that your neighbors are very appreciative of your work. Think of ways to make the yard work more enjoyable, such as starting earlier in the day or listening to music while you work. Quitting should be the last resort.

Build your mental endurance now. It will help prepare you for challenges you may face later.

Find the area of each figure.

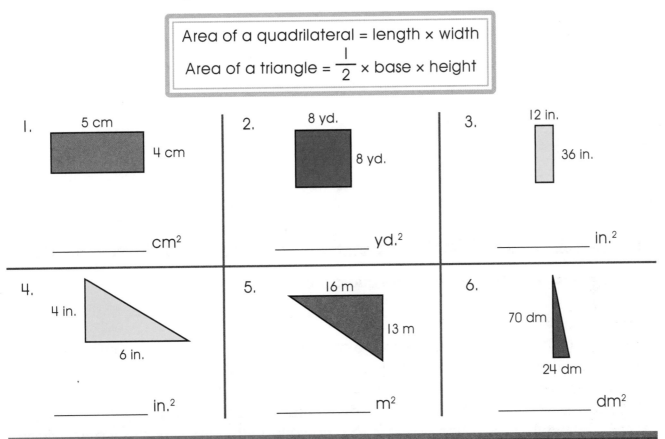

Area of a quadrilateral = length × width

Area of a triangle = $\frac{1}{2}$ × base × height

1. 5 cm

4 cm

_____ cm²

2. 8 yd.

8 yd.

_____ yd.²

3. 12 in.

36 in.

_____ in.²

4. 4 in.

6 in.

_____ in.²

5. 16 m

13 m

_____ m²

6. 70 dm

24 dm

_____ dm²

Correct the paragraph. Draw three lines under each letter that needs to be capitalized.

Pamela's Family

Pamela's family came to the United States from Italy during the industrial revolution. her family worked hard and built a business. They lost their money in the great depression, but they did not give up. Pamela's grandfather is a retired professor, and her mother is a doctor. Last week, governor Taylor and mayor Spenser came to participate in the city's annual immigrant's Day Parade. There were english, french, Russian, german, and scandinavian floats. Pamela and her mother rode on the italian float with father Thomas. Some popular players from the spartans, a local hockey team, were there too. The float depicted the mathematician and pioneer astronomer Galileo gazing at mars through a telescope.

Write the words from the word bank in alphabetical order.

hurried	journey	reunite	enemy
deciding	individual	subscription	toil
alleys	toiletry	identify	victorious

7. _____

8. _____

9. _____

10. _____

11. _____

12. _____

13. _____

14. _____

15. _____

16. _____

17. _____

18. _____

Read the passage. Then, answer the questions.

Sacagawea

The U.S. gold dollar coin shows the image of a young American Indian woman named Sacagawea and her baby. In 1800, when Sacagawea was about 12 years old, an enemy tribe captured her. They took her far away from her Shoshone home. Four years later, Sacagawea joined a group of explorers who wanted to find a way to the Pacific Ocean. Meriwether Lewis and William Clark would lead the group across the American Northwest. Sacagawea went with her husband. Her baby son was strapped to her back. She was the only woman in the group of explorers.

Sacagawea helped make the trip a success. In May of 1805, she jumped into the river to save the explorers' journals that had fallen out of the canoe. Sacagawea found edible plants for the men and acted as interpreter when they met different tribes of American Indians. In August of 1805, the explorers came upon a group of Shoshones. The chief was Sacagawea's brother, whom she had not seen in five years. The tribe gave the explorers the food, guides, and horses they needed to finish their journey and to return home safely. Sacagawea had helped them greatly.

19. What is the main idea of the second paragraph?

    A. Sacagawea helped the explorers survive.

    B. The explorers made discoveries during exploration.

    C. Sacagawea saw the Pacific Ocean.

20. What area did Lewis and Clark plan to explore? _____

FACTOID: An elephant seal can hold its breath for up to two hours.

To find the circumference of a circle, multiply its diameter by *pi*, or 3.14. Fill in the missing information to complete the table.

Radius	Diameter	Circumference
EXAMPLE: 12 mm	**24 mm**	**75.36 mm**
1. 11 in.	22 in.	
2.	18 cm	
3. 10 m		
4. 13 yd.		
5.		150.72 ft.
6.	42 in.	
7. 17 cm		
8.		282.60 mm
9.		314 in.

Add a question mark to the end of each interrogative sentence. Add an exclamation point to the end of each exclamatory sentence.

10.   Do you know how many teeth an adult human has

11.   Does he have 32 teeth

12.   Did you realize that zebras have teeth like rats

13.   Hey! You must be kidding

14.   Wow! Zebras grind down their teeth by eating 15 hours a day

15.   Can their teeth keep growing like rodents' teeth

16.   That is amazing

17.   Is it true that great white sharks have razor-sharp teeth

DAY 2

Look up the word *dramatize* in a dictionary. Then, answer the questions.

18.   What are the guide words on the page? _____

19.   How many meanings are listed for *dramatize*? _____

20.   Write the word. Write the pronunciation. _____

21.   How many syllables does the word have? _____

22.   What does *dramatize* mean in this sentence?

      Do you always have to <u>dramatize</u>, Annie?

      _____

23.   Write the other forms of the word given in the dictionary and tell what part of

      speech they are. _____

24.   List two words on the same page as *dramatize*. Write their pronunciations.

      _____

Pretend that you live in the year 2028. How will life be different? How will you look? What will you eat? How will you get around? Write a detailed paragraph and draw a picture on a separate sheet of paper to describe and show what you imagine.

_____

_____

_____

_____

_____

_____

_____

FITNESS FLASH: Jog in place for 30 seconds.

* See page ii.

Write a word or number from the word bank to complete each sentence.

90	180	acute	angle	vertex
degree	obtuse	protractor	right	

When two rays share an endpoint, they form an (1.) _____ . This

endpoint is called the (2.) _____ of the angle.

The (3.) _____ is the unit used for measuring angles.

A (4.) _____ is used to measure angles. A protractor is marked with

(5.) _____ degrees. You place the center of the protractor on the

vertex of the angle. A (6.) _____ angle looks like a square corner.

It measures (7.) _____ degrees. An (8.) _____

angle is smaller than a right angle, or less than 90 degrees. An (9.) _____

angle is larger than a right angle, or greater than 90 degrees.

Write *right*, *acute*, or *obtuse* to label each angle

10. _____   11. _____   12. _____

Punctuate each date, city and state, city and province, greeting, or closing correctly.

13. Edmond Alberta

_____

15. Dear Grandma

_____

17. Yours truly

_____

19. October 9 2015

_____

14. North Branch New York

_____

16. Dear Uncle Gerald

_____

18. March 3 2010

_____

20. Fall Leaf KS

_____

DAY 3

Read the passage. Then, answer the questions.

The Post Office

In the United States and Canada, the post office is where people buy stamps and mail letters and packages. Postal employees sort mail by region and send it out for delivery on foot, by car, by truck, or by airplane. A country's national post office sets the rates for mailing materials. The cost of postage depends on the size and weight of an item, the distance to its destination, and its target delivery date. Sending the items to arrive the next day costs more than sending them by general delivery, which may take days or weeks. Some post offices offer services such as processing passport applications, banking, and selling greeting cards. Canada Post, the postal service in Canada, is run by the government. The U.S. Postal Service is part of the executive branch of the government but is run independently. Both government postal organizations face competition from private postal companies that may offer faster mail delivery at a lower cost.

21. What is the main idea of this passage?
    A. Mail is sorted by region.
    B. The Canadian postal service is called Canada Post.
    C. The post office is important for communicating by mail.

22. Why do people visit post offices? _____

    _____

23. How do postal employees deliver mail? _____

    _____

24. Who determines the rates for mailing materials? _____

    _____

25. What does the cost of postage depend on? _____

    _____

FACTOID: Approximately 2,000 thunderstorms are happening around the world right now.

Use a protractor to measure each angle.

1.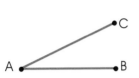

2.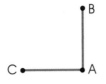

3.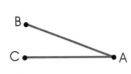

4.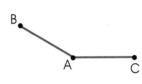

_____ _____ _____ _____

Use a protractor to draw an angle for each measure.

5. 75°

6. 60°

7. 15°

Are the commas in each sentence used correctly? Write *yes* or *no*.

8.   The Smiths visited Philadelphia, Pennsylvania and New, York. _____

9.   They saw museums, of art, history and science in Philadelphia. _____

10. Don, Debbie, and Dan toured Independence Hall. _____

Write commas where they are needed in each sentence.

11. Debbie Don and Dan were impressed with New York City.

12. It is an important business cultural and trade center.

13. The Bronx Manhattan Queens Brooklyn and Staten Island are its five boroughs.

14. Chinatown Greenwich Village and Harlem are three neighborhoods
     in Manhattan.

15. The Smiths saw Times Square Rockefeller Center and the United
     Nations Headquarters.

DAY 4

Write *yes* or *no to* answer each question. Use a dictionary if you need help.

16. Is a *gizzard* a kind of bird? _____

17. Would a boy wear a *mukluk*? _____

18. Could you work as a *gofer*? _____

19. Do you wear a *goatee* on your arm? _____

20. Could you play with a *googol*? _____

21. Is a *truffle* a rich chocolate candy? _____

22. Could you plant a *vetch*? _____

23. Does *yep* mean yes? _____

24. Is a *yeti* mysterious? _____

25. Could animals be kept in a *scribe*? _____

26. Is an *orlop* deck part of a ship? _____

27. Can you live in a *yurt*? _____

28. Would you chop wood with an *italic*? _____

29. Could you eat a *mango*? _____

30. Can you drive an *osier*? _____

Climbing to Endurance

Climbing stairs is an easy way to improve your endurance, and this activity can be done almost anywhere. Head to a gymnasium, stadium, office, or apartment building and find several flights of stairs. Begin by walking up the stairs. Be careful to place your foot firmly on each stair, hold on to the railing, and watch out for people who may be descending. For a challenge, or as your endurance improves, wear a backpack filled with several books as you climb your way to improved endurance.

FITNESS FLASH: Hop on your right foot for 30 seconds.

* See page ii.

To find the volume of a rectangular solid, multiply the length, width, and height of the solid. Find the volume of each figure.

1.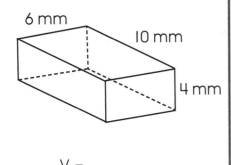

   5 m   2 m   6 m

   V = _____

2.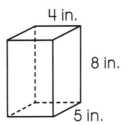

   4 in.   8 in.   5 in.

   V = _____

3.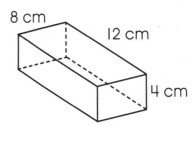

   4.6 m   2.9 m   3.1 m

   V = _____

4.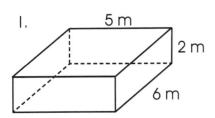

   6 mm   10 mm   4 mm

   V = _____

5.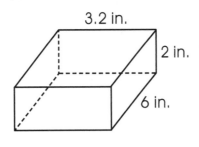

   3.2 in.   2 in.   6 in.

   V = _____

6. 8 cm   12 cm   4 cm

   V = _____

Quotation marks are used before and after a person's exact words, around the titles of short stories, poems, and songs, and around the titles of magazine and newspaper articles. Add quotation marks where they belong in each sentence.

7. Robert asked, What are the rules for this game?

8. Mother was making lunch when Jay came home. Please set the table, she said.

9. What's that terrible noise? cried Carla.

10. Cindy was playing Tennessee Waltz on her guitar when Pedro came in.

11. I don't think that I can do this by myself, Marge sighed.

12. Hillary is singing America the Beautiful to her sister.

13. Do you like baseball or football better? Debra asked. I like baseball better.

14. Not me, answered Eleanor. I like basketball best.

DAY 5

Write an X beside the word or phrase that is a synonym for the first word in each list. Use a thesaurus if you need help.

15. **bronco**

_____ panther

_____ horse

_____ insect

16. **fanfare**

_____ explanation

_____ metal

_____ music

17. **residence**

_____ payment

_____ home

_____ disease

18. **narrative**

_____ complaint

_____ length

_____ story

19. **sapling**

_____ young plant

_____ vitamin

_____ young tree

20. **attire**

_____ medal

_____ wisdom

_____ clothing

- The *range* is the difference between the highest and lowest number in a set of data.
- To calculate the *mean* (or average), add the list of numbers and divide by the number of items.
- The *median* is the middle number that appears in the data when it is arranged in numeric order.
- The *mode* is the number that appears most often in the data.

Use the chart to answer the questions about the number of medals awarded at the 2000 Summer Olympic Games held in Sydney, Australia.

21. What is the range of the data?

_____

22. What is the mode of the data?

_____

23. What is the median of the data?

_____

24. What is the mean number of medals awarded? _____

Country	Number of Medals
United States	91
Russia	88
China	59
Australia	58
Germany	56
Italy	34
Cuba	29
Great Britain	28
South Korea	28

CHARACTER CHECK: Talk with an adult about someone you know who shows determination.

Compare each pair of figures. Write *congruent* or *similar*.

1.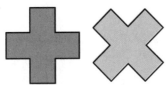

_____

2.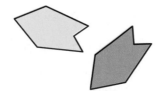

_____

3.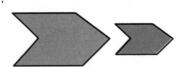

_____

4.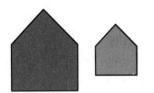

_____

5.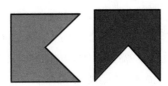

_____

6.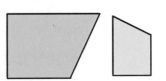

_____

Write each number or fraction in word form.

7. 87

_____

8. 39

_____

9. 43

_____

10. $\dfrac{1}{2}$

_____

11. $\dfrac{9}{10}$

_____

12. $\dfrac{3}{4}$

_____

13. 292

_____

14. 781

_____

DAY 6

Read the passage. Then, answer the questions.

North American Pioneers

Many early North American pioneers came from Europe. Some came to pursue religious freedom, while others wanted more land for their families. Many settlers built villages along the shores of lakes, rivers, and the ocean. Water was important not only for drinking, farming, and washing clothes, but also for powering mills and traveling to other settlements. Most pioneers worked as farmers. They had to clear the land of trees before they could plant many crops. Pioneers also raised horses and oxen to help pull wagons and sheep to provide wool. When there were enough children in a village, parents sometimes built a schoolhouse and hired a teacher. Usually, all of the children were taught in a single room. Otherwise, children might be educated at home. As villages grew in size, they sometimes built a doctor's office, a blacksmith's shop, and a general store where goods were sold.

15. What is the main idea of this passage?
    A. Some pioneers came from Europe.
    B. Pioneer children sometimes studied at home.
    C. Most early pioneers were farmers who lived in small villages.

16. Why did the early pioneers come to North America? _____

    _____

17. Which animals did pioneers often raise? _____

    _____

18. How were pioneer children educated? _____

    _____

19. What other buildings might a pioneer village include? _____

    _____

FACTOID: Seventy percent of Earth's surface is water.

12 inches (in.) = 1 foot (ft.)
3 ft. = 1 yard (yd.)

Convert each measurement.

1. 12 in. = _____ ft.   2. 18 in. = _____ ft.   3. 2 ft. = _____ in.

4. 48 in. = _____ ft.   5. 6 ft. = _____ yd.   6. 7 yd. = _____ ft.

7. 1 yd. = _____ in.   8. 9 ft. = _____ yd.   9. 3 yd. = _____ ft.

10. 6 in. = _____ ft.   11. 10 yd. = _____ ft.   12. 11 ft. = _____ in.

Circle the verb in parentheses that agrees with the subject of each sentence.

13. People (use, uses) various kinds of watercraft for fun.

14. Old-fashioned muscle power (propel, propels) some types of watercraft.

15. Some rafts (is, are) made by tying pieces of wood together.

16. Pacific Islanders (digs, dig) out tree trunks to make dugout canoes.

17. The world's largest dugout canoe (carry, carries) 70 people.

18. Boys and girls often (enjoy, enjoys) canoeing at summer camps.

19. One paddler (steer, steers) a type of canoe called a kayak.

20. The paddle (is, are) double-bladed.

Read the partial table of contents and index from a history book. Then, answer the questions.

Table of Contents

Index

21. What is the difference between the table of contents and the index in a book?

     _____

     _____

22. If you wanted to see if there was a picture of Andrew Jackson in the book,

     where would you look? _____

23. Where would you look to find out who fought in the Civil War? _____

     _____

24. How many sections are in Chapter Five? _____

25. On what page could you look to learn who Massasoit was? _____

FITNESS FLASH: Hop on your left foot 10 times.

* See page ii.

I kilometer (km) = 1,000 meters (m)	10 dm = 100 centimeters (cm)
I m = 10 decimeters (dm)	100 cm = 1,000 millimeters (mm)

Convert each measurement.

1. 25 cm = _250_ mm
2. 3 m = _____ mm
3. 9 dm = _____ mm

4. 10 dm = _1000_ mm
5. 12 m = _____ mm
6. 8 m = _____ cm

7. 50 mm = _____ cm
8. 100 m = _____ cm
9. 4 km = _____ cm

Correct the subject/verb agreement errors in the passage.

Every Monday, students in Mrs. Verdan's class works with partners to complete math challenges. Each pair select its own work space. Jeremy and Melvin goes to the math center. Gregory and Leo likes the sunny table by the window. Hector and Jeff chooses chairs near the board. Lily and Masandra takes the round table near the door. Manny and Zoe grabs the soft seats in the library corner. Macon and Travis sits near the science center. All of the pairs has 45 minutes to solve the day's puzzle. Most of them finishes on time. They shares their solutions with the whole group. A few students meets with Mrs. Verdan after school. She explain the solutions and answer questions. Mrs. Verdan's students always enjoys the weekly math challenges.

DAY 8

Read the following passage. Then, answer the questions.

Timbuktu

Timbuktu is a small trading town in central Mali, located near the southern edge of the Sahara Desert. Established around AD 1100, it was a trading post for products from North and West Africa. Northern camel caravans traded salt, cloth, cowrie shells, and copper for gold, kola nuts, ivory, and slaves who came from the south.

Timbuktu's location left it open to attack, and control of the city changed many times. It has been ruled by the Mali Empire, the Songhai Empire, Morocco, nomads, France, and others. It is not as important or populated as it once was. Many of its mud and brick buildings are eroding and are half buried in the sand.

10. Underline the topic sentence of the passage.

11. Circle the main idea of the first paragraph.

12. Circle the main idea of the second paragraph.

Research the Trail of Tears. Write an acrostic poem about this event using a letter of "Trail of Tears" to begin each line.

T _____

R _____

A _____

I _____

L _____

O _____

F _____

T _____

E _____

A _____

R _____

S _____

FACTOID: A human brain has an average of 100 billion nerve cells.

16 ounces (oz.) = 1 pound (lb.)
2,000 lb. = 1 ton

2 cups = 1 pint (pt.)
2 pt. = 1 quart (qt.)
8 pt. = 1 gallon (gal.)

Convert each measurement.

1. 32 oz. = _____ lb.

2. 3 lb. = _____ oz.

3. 8 oz. = _____ lb.

4. 4 oz. = _____ lb.

5. 1 ton = _____ lb.

6. 4,000 lb. = _____ tons

7. 2 cups = _____ pt.

8. 3 pt. = _____ cups

9. 2 pt. = _____ qt.

10. 4 qt. = _____ gal.

11. 8 pt. = _____ gal.

12. 1 cup = _____ gal.

Rewrite the friendly letter. Use the correct form, punctuation marks, and capitalization. Be sure to indent each paragraph.

1624 bay lane short creek pa 12525 may 10 2009 dear aunt ann and uncle james school will soon be out for the summer i am looking forward to it the year was good and i learned a lot mom and dad are going to france in july i don't want to go with them I'm writing this letter to ask if i can stay with you july 10 through July 22 i would love to help you take care of the horses and do anything else that you would want me to do i would also help around the house please let me know if i can come your loving niece julie ann

_____

_____

_____

_____

_____

_____

_____

DAY 9

Read the passage. Then, answer the questions.

Gwendolyn Brooks

Gwendolyn Brooks began writing poems when she was seven years old. When her parents saw how much she loved to work with words, they set up a desk for her and told her that she could write instead of doing chores in the house.

Although the Brooks family was poor, they felt rich because they were happy. Later, Brooks wrote about families like hers. These people lived in the city and did not have much money. Sometimes, they did not have enough to eat. But, they loved life.

By the age of 16, Brooks had published 75 poems. At 25, she won her first writing award. She published her first book of poems, *A Street in Bronzeville*, in 1945. They were poems about people who lived in the part of Chicago, Illinois, where Brooks lived.

In 1949, Brooks published *Annie Allen*, a book of poems that won her the Pulitzer Prize. Brooks was the first African American to earn this prestigious writing prize. Later, Brooks taught writing at colleges and worked for the Library of Congress.

Brooks wrote some poems about brave people working for equal rights. She wrote about the lives of Southern African Americans as well as life around her in the city. She said that she was like a newspaper writer, reporting the things going on around her.

13. Number the events in the order in which they happened.

_____ Brooks wrote *Annie Allen*.

_____ Brooks's parents set up a desk for her so that she could write.

_____ Brooks published her first book of poems.

_____ Brooks worked for the Library of Congress.

14. What big award did Brooks win? _____

15. Whom did Brooks write about in most of her poems? _____

_____

16. Why is it especially important that Brooks won the Pulitzer Prize?
    A. She was the first poet to win the award.
    B. She was the first woman to win the award.
    C. She was the first African American to win the award.

FITNESS FLASH: Do 10 jumping jacks.

* See page ii.

| I liter (L) = 1,000 milliliter (mL) | I gram (g) = 1,000 milligram (mg) |
| I kiloliter (kL) = 1,000 L | I kilogram (kg) = 1,000 g |

Convert each measurement.

1. 1,000 mL = _____ L

2. 1,000 L = _____ kL

3. 4 L = _____ mL

4. 5 kL = _____ L

5. 3,000 mL = _____ L

6. 9 L = _____ mL

7. 8 kg = _____ g

8. 4,000 mg = _____ g

9. 9.5 g = _____ mg

10. 2 kg = _____ mg

11. 9,000 g = _____ kg

12. 7 kg = _____ mg

Address the envelope for Juan's letter. Be sure to write the addresses on the envelope in the correct places. Use uppercase letters and punctuation marks where they belong.

Juan Roberts
1624 bay lane
short creek pa 12526

mr barry york and mrs melinda york
1010 sunset ranch rd
ely id 89621

DAY 10

Write a topic sentence for each paragraph. Try to make each topic sentence interesting so that others will want to read the paragraph.

13. They are among the world's oldest and largest living things. Some are thousands of years old and more than 200 feet (61 m) tall. Some are 100 feet (30.5 m) around at the base. They are the giant sequoia and redwood trees of California and Oregon.

    _____

14. It can be a great work, like a Michelangelo carving or an African mask. It can be very large, like the Statue of Liberty, or small enough to place on a table and hold in your hand. It has always played an important part in the history of humanity. Sculpture is an excellent way to express your ideas and feelings.

    _____

The rock cycle illustrates three types of changes in rocks. Write the correct phrase from the word bank on each numbered arrow. Each phrase will be used twice.

heating and pressure	melting and crystallization	sedimentation and compaction

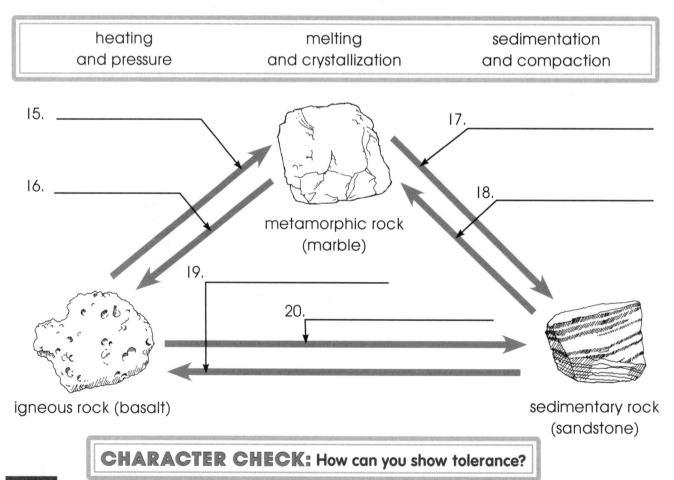

15. _____

16. _____

17. _____

18. _____

19. _____

20. _____

metamorphic rock (marble)

igneous rock (basalt)

sedimentary rock (sandstone)

CHARACTER CHECK: How can you show tolerance?

Percentage is the comparison of a number to 100. Write each ratio as a percentage.

EXAMPLE: $\frac{15}{100}$ = 15%   15 to 100 = 15%   15:100 = 15%

1. $\frac{20}{100}$ = _____

2. $\frac{50}{100}$ = _____

3. 8:100 = _____

4. 47:100 = _____

5. 9 to 100 = _____

Write each percentage as a fraction.

6. 19% = _____

7. 24% = _____

8. 87% = _____

9. 36% = _____

10. 99% = _____

Write each percentage as a fraction. Simplify each fraction.

11. 50% = _____

12. 90% = _____

13. 20% = _____

14. 45% = _____

15. 70% = _____

Write the correct past-tense form of each irregular verb in parentheses to complete each sentence.

16. Phil (read) _____ about Pelé, one of the greatest soccer players of all time.

17. Pelé (grow) _____ up in Brazil.

18. He (begin) _____ playing professional soccer in 1956.

19. Pelé (hold) _____ every scoring record in Brazil.

20. His team (win) _____ five South American Championships.

21. Pelé (lead) _____ his team to three World Cup championships.

22. Pelé (leave) _____ his Brazilian team after 18 years.

23. He (go) _____ to the United States in 1975 to play for New York.

DAY II

Context clues help you learn new words and their meanings. Use the context clues in each sentence to tell what the underlined word means.

24. Mary <u>feigned</u> surprise when her friends had a birthday party for her.

   _____

25. My <u>colleagues</u> and I work together on many new projects.

   _____

26. Maurice looks at his watch often to make sure that he is always <u>punctual</u>.

   _____

27. Joseph, a <u>philatelist</u>, has a large collection of stamps.

   _____

28. The dog napping in the shade was hardly able to <u>bestir</u> herself for dinner.

   _____

Number the steps in the order in which they happen. The steps describe how a bill becomes a law in the United States.

   _____ Get the president's approval.

   _____ Write a bill.

   _____ Get a majority vote in Congress.

   _____ If the president vetoes the bill, it may become a law by a two-thirds majority vote in Congress.

Now, create a bill that you think should become a law. Explain why you think that it is needed. On a separate sheet of paper, draw a comic strip that shows characters putting these steps into action.

FACTOID: The great pyramids at Giza were built about 4,500 years ago.

Decimals that name hundreds can easily be written as percentages because percent means "per hundred." Write a percentage and a decimal for the shaded area of each picture.

1.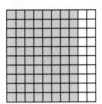

2.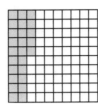

3.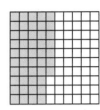

_____   _____   _____

Write each percentage as a decimal.

4. 27% = _____   5. 35% = _____   6. 54% = _____   7. 43% = _____

Write each decimal as a percentage.

8. 0.15 = _____   9. 0.88 = _____   10. 0.07 = _____   11. 0.91 = _____

Circle the noun or verb in parentheses that makes the information in each sentence more specific.

12. Chimpanzees live in (regions, parts) of Africa where jungle vegetation is plentiful.

13. They (hold, grip) tree branches with their palms and long fingers.

14. These (animals, primates) climb trees easily.

15. Chimpanzees eat a variety of foods, including (termites, bugs).

16. If a chimpanzee wants to eat termites, she (pokes, puts) a twig into the center of a termite mound.

17. Then, she removes the twig and (plucks, takes) off the termites.

18. If a male chimpanzee is agitated, he might (run, charge) down a hill, (taking, ripping) off tree branches.

19. He will beat the ground as he (bounds, walks) through the grass.

Read the passage. Then, answer the questions.

Geologists

Geology is the branch of science that deals with Earth's materials and structure. Geologists study processes such as the movement of plates on the planet's crust, volcanic eruptions, and earthquakes. Learning about these events can help scientists predict how Earth might change in the future. Some geologists study the soil to help plants grow better. Farmers can adjust the minerals in their soil to produce bigger crops. Studying water drainage helps scientists learn how to prevent flooding. Some geologists study the makeup of the sea floor, and others research gemstones. Geologists study the movement of glaciers and the use of natural resources, such as oil and gas. Many geologists collect data in the field for weeks or months and return to the laboratory to interpret their data. Geologists can be found in almost every location on Earth.

20. What is the main idea of this passage?
    A. Geologists study the materials and structure of Earth.
    B. Some geologists study the soil to help plants grow better.
    C. Geologists learn about different landforms.

21. What does geology deal with? _____

    _____

22. Which processes do geologists study? _____

    _____

    _____

23. Why do geologists study soil? _____

    _____

24. What do geologists do in laboratories? _____

    _____

FITNESS FLASH: Jog in place for 30 seconds.

* See page ii.

Bar graphs help you compare data at a glance. Answer the questions about the bar graph.

Valley Fair Music Place kept track of the different types of music it sold during the summer months.

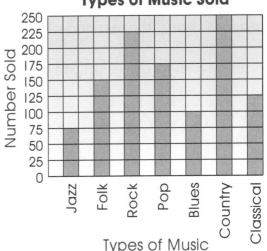

Types of Music Sold

1. Which type of music was the most popular?

   _____

2. Which sold the least? _____

   _____

3. What is the difference between the greatest and the least number sold? _____

4. What is the average number of music sold?

   _____

5. Which is your favorite type of music? _____

Circle the word in parentheses that makes each sentence more descriptive.

6. The concert hall was (big, gigantic).

7. It was (ornately, nicely) decorated in red velvet and gold.

8. The (audience, people) waited eagerly for the concert to begin.

9. The (young, thirty-year-old) conductor raised his baton.

10. The (big, enormous) orchestra came to attention.

11. The audience was (very, completely) still.

12. The orchestra performed (magnificently, well).

13. The tenor sang (nicely, brilliantly).

14. The audience clapped (enthusiastically, loudly).

15. It was a (good, splendid) concert.

Some key words and punctuation marks signal that an author is giving context clues. Write what the underlined word means in each sentence. Then, write the type of signal that helped you determine the word's meaning. Signals include commas, dashes, parentheses, and phrases such as *which is* and *in other words*.)

16.   I feel <u>torpid</u>—sluggish and lazy—in the hot summer weather.

_____

17.   Paul Bunyan used an <u>adze</u>, which is a flat-bladed ax, to cut down the forest.

_____

18.   The cook made <u>ragout</u>, a highly seasoned stew, every day for the ranch hands.

_____

19.   Jason smashed his <u>patella</u>, in other words, his kneecap.

_____

20.   David can play a <u>marimba</u> (a xylophone).

_____

Discovering Perseverance

Perseverance means to keep going even if something is difficult and there are obstacles to overcome. Talk with a family member about the quality of perseverance and discuss friends, family members, or neighbors who have demonstrated this quality in their lives. Then, ask one of the individuals whose name was mentioned if you can conduct an interview with him. During the interview, ask this person specific questions to help you better understand the challenges he overcame to become successful. After the interview, make a three-panel comic strip highlighting a before, a during, and an after scene. In each panel, be sure to include an appropriate quote for that stage of the person's quest: first in getting started, then in never giving up, etc. When the comic strip is completed, schedule a time to meet with the person, sharing the comic strip as well as what you learned from this experience.

FACTOID: Australia's Great Barrier Reef can be seen from outer space.

Pie charts compare parts of a whole. Answer each question about the pie chart.

Jake earns $20 a week doing chores for his neighbors. The pie chart shows how he uses his money.

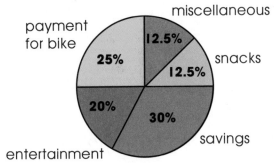

1. How much money does Jake spend on snacks each week? $ _____

2. How much does he spend on entertainment each week? $ _____

3. How much does he spend paying off his bike each week? $ _____

4. How much does he save each week? $ _____

Contractions containing *not* are called negatives. Words such as *nothing*, *nobody*, and *never* are also negatives. You should not use double negatives in writing or in speaking. Underline the double negatives in each sentence. Then, rewrite the sentence correctly.

EXAMPLE: The fight <u>didn't</u> solve <u>nothing</u>.

   The fight didn't solve anything.

5.   The team didn't want no trouble.

   _____

6.   Haven't you never seen Yellowstone National Park?

   _____

7.   There aren't no eggs in the carton.

   _____

8.   He wasn't near no base when he was tagged out.

   _____

9.   There isn't no way to get there from here.

   _____

10.   The explanation didn't make no sense.

   _____

Circle the situation that led to the ending described in each sentence.

11. Finally, a taxi pulled over to the curb, and the traveler climbed in with his drenched suitcase.
    A. The traveler had just arrived.
    B. The traveler had called for a taxi.
    C. The traveler had been standing in the rain trying to hail a taxi.

12. Mickey left the doctor's office with her arm in a sling.
    A. Mickey had gone to the doctor to get some new medicine.
    B. Mickey had gone to the doctor because she had tripped and fallen on her shoulder.
    C. Mickey had gone to the doctor because the sling was uncomfortable.

13. No one was being served in the cafeteria line.
    A. The server had gone to refill the chicken tray.
    B. The food was very good.
    C. There were too many people in line.

Match each word with its definition. Use a dictionary, a science book, or the Internet if you need help.

14. _____ asteroids

A. an object that orbits a planet or a moon

15. _____ comet

B. rocky or metal objects that orbit the sun in a belt between Mars and Jupiter; also called planetoids or minor planets

16. _____ star

C. a huge ball of glowing gas that can exist for billions of years; our sun is the closest one

17. _____ satellite

D. a small object orbiting the sun that is made of frozen ice, gas, and dust; it has a tail that always points away from the sun

18. _____ planet

E. a large body that orbits a star and does not produce its own light; there are eight in our solar system

FITNESS FLASH: Hop on your left foot 10 times.

* See page ii.

A pictograph uses picture symbols to represent different amounts of data or specific units. Answer each question about the pictograph.

School Visitors

Monday	🚶 🚶 🚶 🚶 🚶 🚶 🚶 🚶
Tuesday	🚶 🚶 🚶 🚶 🚶 🚶
Wednesday	🚶 🚶 🚶
Thursday	🚶 🚶 🚶
Friday	🚶 🚶 🚶 🚶 🚶 🚶

🚶 = 10 family members

Riverton School kept track of how many family members visited their school during Family Week. They made a pictograph to show the students the results.

1. When did most family members visit? _____

2. What does 🚶 mean? _____

3. How many family members visited the school during Family Week? _____

4. When did the least number of family members visit? _____

5. How many family members visited on Friday? _____

6. What other type of graph could have been used to show this data? _____

_____

Underline the double negatives in each sentence. Then, rewrite the sentence correctly.

7.   Can't no one solve the puzzle? _____

8.   Rick didn't have nothing to read._____

9.   Annie hadn't never seen that._____

10. Don't spill none of the juice._____

11. There isn't nothing you can do about it. _____

_____

David Glasgow Farragut

At age nine, David Glasgow Farragut went to sea. Farragut's father, who was Spanish, came to the United States in 1776. He fought for his new country in the American Revolution and the War of 1812. Farragut's mother died when he was seven, so he was sent to live with naval captain David Porter. Porter found a place on a ship for Farragut.

Farragut was at sea during the War of 1812. When he was 12 years old, he was put in charge of a prize ship that had been captured from the enemy. Farragut's job was to get the ship safely to port. This was a hard job during a war, but Farragut did it.

After many years of peace, the Civil War began. Farragut loved his home in Virginia, but he told his wife that he was "sticking to the flag." So, the couple moved to New York. David Farragut was 60 years old.

The Mississippi River was guarded too well for the North to use it. Farragut was asked to **capture** New Orleans, Louisiana. It was an important port for the South and the gateway to the huge river system. Farragut took his flagship, the *Hartford*, and almost 50 other ships with him. He captured New Orleans and other cities on the Mississippi. Finally, in 1864, he turned to Mobile, Alabama. Under heavy fire, Farragut captured Mobile, the South's last big port.

In less than two years, the *Hartford* had been hit 240 times by cannon fire. The war was almost over. Farragut went home to New York. Farragut was made an admiral for the important work he did during the Civil War.

12. What does the word *capture* mean in the passage?
    A. to take control of
    B. to guard
    C. to keep safe
    D. to clothe

13. Number the events in the order in which they happened.

    _____ Farragut brought a captured ship safely to port.

    _____ Farragut captured the port of Mobile, Alabama.

    _____ Farragut was sent to live with a navy captain.

    _____ Farragut fought battles on the Mississippi River.

14. What city did Farragut have to capture to get to the Mississippi River? _____

15. What rank was Farragut given at the end of the war? _____

CHARACTER CHECK: Make a list of three things you can do at home that demonstrate cooperation. Share your list with a family member.

Clayton's mother bought him some new clothes for camp. She bought him four pairs of shorts—red, green, blue, and black. She also bought him four shirts—orange, yellow, brown, and white.

I. Use the tree diagram to organize the data. How many different combinations of shorts and shirts can Clayton wear? _____

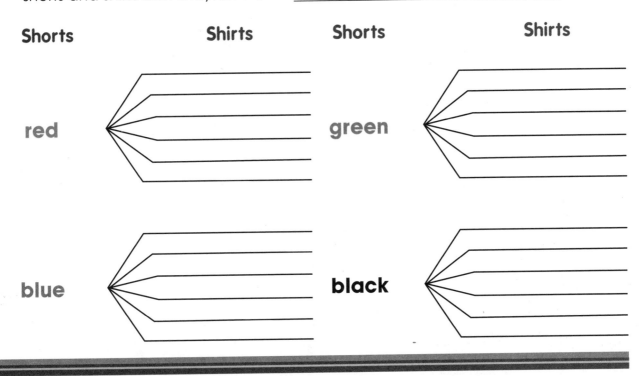

Correct the paragraph. Draw three lines under each letter that needs to be capitalized. Cross out each misspelled word and write the correct spelling above the word. Add punctuation where needed.

today the term "American Indian" is used to describe people indigenous to america.

however the firt explorers who came to America referred to them as "Indians"

unknown to the explorers, most tribes had their own names. for example the name

used by the deleware indians of eastern north america meant "genuine men." the

Indians' languages ways of life, and homes wer all very different. The aztic and maya

Indians of central america built large citys The apache and Paiute used brushes and

mating to make simple huts the plains indians buit coneshaped tepees covered with

buffalo skns Cliff dwellers and other Pueblo groups usd sun-dried bricks to make

many-storyed houses

DAY 16

Some sentences have clue words or transition words that help show cause-and-effect relationships. Complete each sentence with a clue word or transition word. Then, write the cause and effect.

EXAMPLE: Our school was closed today <u>because</u> of the snowstorm we had last night.
Cause: snowstorm
Effect: school was closed

2. It snowed all day, _____ the ground was white.

   Cause: _____

   Effect: _____

3. Our electricity went out last night, _____ we went out to dinner.

   Cause: _____

   Effect: _____

4. Joe left the gate unlatched, _____ all of the cattle were out in the road.

   Cause: _____

   Effect: _____

5. Scott woke up with the flu today, _____ he had to miss school.

   Cause: _____

   Effect: _____

Pollution is a problem that affects all living things on Earth. Match each term with its description.

6. _____ leaked oil from a tanker that ran aground   A. greenhouse effect

7. _____ poisonous materials such as paint thinner   B. hazardous waste

8. _____ smoke and exhaust that mix with water vapor   C. acid rain

9. _____ a warming of the surface and lower atmosphere of Earth   D. oil spill

FACTOID: Hummingbirds can fly up to 60 miles (96.5 km) per hour.

Find the probability of the spinner landing on each color.

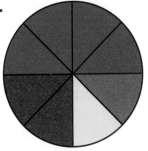

1. red _____
2. green _____
3. blue _____
4. yellow _____

Find the probability of picking each letter out of the word *possibility* in the box.

5. s _____
6. b _____
7. p _____
8. x _____
9. i _____
10. y _____

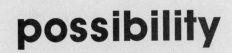

possibility

Use the common predicates or subjects in each group of sentences to write a single sentence.

11. Jim liked to visit Grandma and Grandpa. Sean liked to visit Grandma and Grandpa. Maria liked to visit Grandma and Grandpa.

_____

_____

12. Grandpa had horses on his farm. Grandpa had cows on his farm. Grandpa had goats on his farm.

_____

13. Grandma raised chickens. Grandma raised ducks. Grandma raised geese.

_____

14. Daisies grew in her garden. Tulips grew in her garden. Roses grew in her garden.

_____

DAY 17

Write an effect to complete each sentence. Look for clue words or transition words.

EXAMPLE: (cause) The old house had not been painted in years,
(effect) so the first thing we did was paint it. (The clue word is *so*.)

15. The oven temperature was too high, so _____ .

16. _____ because my new shoes were too tight.

17. The wind was blowing hard, so _____ .

18. Because I didn't get up early enough this morning, _____ .

19. _____ because I didn't study.

Write a cause to complete each sentence.

20. The plane was delayed due to _____ .

21. _____ , so my stomach hurt.

22. _____ , so we decided to celebrate.

23. The drinks were very sweet because _____ .

24. _____ , so there was no fruit on the trees this summer.

Skip to Success!

Skipping is a great way to build endurance and improve your speed, agility, and quickness. Find a long, flat surface, such as a sidewalk, driveway, or yard. To begin, skip forward, lifting one knee forward and into the air. At the same time, raise your opposite arm. Concentrate on jumping straight into the air and reaching your arms as high as possible. Skip for 30 seconds, alternating legs. Repeat this 3–5 times. To make this activity more challenging, try skipping for longer periods of time or increasing your number of repetitions.

FITNESS FLASH: Hop on your right foot for 30 seconds.

* See page ii.

Use the Venn diagram to compare each set of data.

1. Mark, Heather, and Charita compared the multiples of 4 and 5.
   Multiples of 4: 0, 4, 8, 12, 16, 20
   Multiples of 5: 0, 5, 10, 15, 20, 25

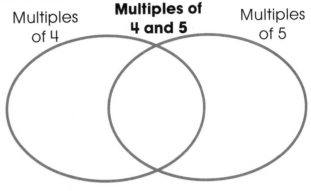

Multiples of 4   **Multiples of 4 and 5**   Multiples of 5

2. Cameron, Sean, and Alexandra compared the diameters of the seeds they found.
   Cameron: 0.5 cm, 1 cm, 1.5 cm, 2 cm
   Sean: 0.5 cm, 1.5 cm, 3 cm, 3.5 cm
   Alexandra: 0.25 cm, 0.5 cm, 2 cm, 3 cm

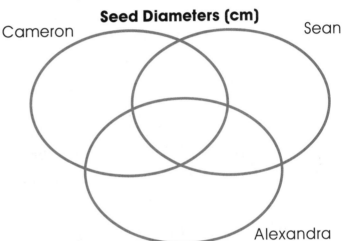

Seed Diameters (cm)
Cameron   Sean   Alexandra

Underline the person being addressed in each sentence.

3. "Walter, you must clean your room today."

4. "I've been waiting for your call, Gerald, since you left two hours ago."

5. "Eli and Tanesha went to the park, Alejandro."

6. "I'm going to watch the movie, Ian."

7. "My room is clean and my homework is done, Dad."

8. "This artwork is exceptional, Betsy."

9. "Since you have been so helpful, Donna, you can call a friend."

10. "Tara, your story is very interesting."

Read the passage. Then, answer the questions.

New England

Six U.S. states make up the area called New England. Massachusetts was founded in 1630 by people who disagreed with the teachings of the Church of England. The first settlers there were Pilgrims, who arrived on the *Mayflower* in 1620. Rhode Island was founded in 1636 by people who left the Massachusetts Bay Colony seeking religious freedom. People who settled in New Hampshire, which was founded in 1638, were looking for a place to fish and trade successfully. People who moved to Connecticut, which was founded in 1636, settled on the fertile farmland along the Connecticut River. Maine was once a part of the Massachusetts Bay Colony but became a separate state under the Missouri Compromise of 1820. Vermont, founded in 1777, was fought over by several colonies and was originally called New Connecticut. Today, New England is famous for many things, including its beautiful autumn foliage and its fishing industry.

11. What is the main idea of this passage?

    A.   Many people in New Hampshire enjoy fishing.

    B.   Massachusetts was founded in 1630.

    C.   New England is a region of the United States.

12. Which states make up the area of New England? _____

_____

_____

13. Why did people settle in Massachusetts and Rhode Island? _____

_____

14. What businesses did people in New Hampshire work in? _____

_____

15. What is New England famous for today? _____

_____

FACTOID: Only one percent of Earth's water is drinkable.

Follow the directions for the coordinate graph.

1. Plot each coordinate pair and label each point. The first one has been done for you.

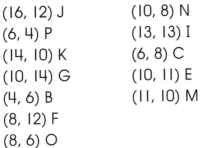

(2, 2) A	(12, 8) L
(12, 16) H	(8, 10) D
(16, 12) J	(10, 8) N
(6, 4) P	(13, 13) I
(14, 10) K	(6, 8) C
(10, 14) G	(10, 11) E
(4, 6) B	(11, 10) M
(8, 12) F	
(8, 6) O	

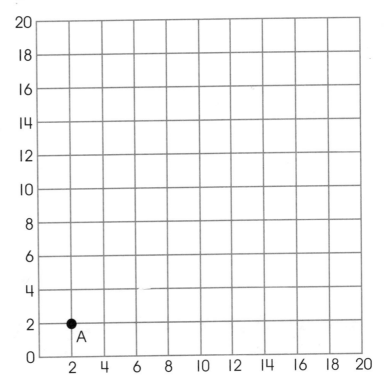

2. Connect points A through P in alphabetical order.

3. Connect point P to point A.

4. Connect point E to point I and point I to point M.

The pronouns *who* and *whom* can be used to ask a question or introduce a clause. *Who* is used when the pronoun is the subject. *Whom* is used when the pronoun is an object. Write *who* or *whom* to complete each sentence.

5. _____ made the first moon landing?

6. _____ do you like the best among the candidates?

7. _____ is your best friend?

8. _____ won the gold medal?

9. _____ does Ryan think will be the best choice for the math contest?

10. _____ was the man she saw walking his dog?

11. _____ shall I call in case of an emergency?

12. He is the person _____ is always late!

13. One of the boys _____ we know is very tall.

14. A teacher _____ we admire spoke at our graduation.

DAY 19

Underline the noun that is being personified in each sentence. Then, write the personifying word or words.

15. The first-place trophy proudly stood on the shelf in Charlie's room.

_____

16. Because we could not go out to play, we watched from our window as the clouds spit icicles.

_____

17. Autumn leaves seemed to sing as they danced across the lawn.

_____

18. Horns honked angrily as drivers became impatient.

_____

19. The sun played hide-and-seek with me as it popped in and out of the clouds.

_____

Because of women like Lucy Stone, Susan B. Anthony, Lucretia Mott, Elizabeth Cady Stanton, and Sarah and Angelina Grimke, women in the United States have many rights today that they didn't have in earlier times. Research one of these women and write an essay about the trials she had to go through because of what she believed.

_____

_____

_____

_____

_____

_____

_____

_____

FITNESS FLASH: Do 10 jumping jacks.

* See page ii.

Roman numerals use letters of the alphabet to represent numbers. Circle the correct Roman numeral for each number written in standard form.

I = 1	V = 5	X = 10	L = 50	C = 100	D = 500	M = 1,000

1.	365	CCCXXXXXIIIII	CCCLXV	CCCDLXV
2.	2,003	MMIIV	MMXII	MMIII
3.	796	DCCXCVI	DCCLXXVI	CCCMLXXXXVI
4.	847	DCCCXLVII	CCMXXXXVII	DCCCXXXXVII
5.	1,742	MCCCMXXXXII	MDCCXLII	MDCCXXXXII
6.	3,491	MMMCDLXXXXI	MMMDCXCI	MMMCDXCI
7.	865	DCXXCIIIII	DCXXCV	DCCCLXV
8.	1,838	MCCMXXXIIV	MDCCCXXXVIII	MMMCCDIIIVIII
9.	2,345	MMCCDXXXXV	MMCCCXLV	MMCCDXLIIIII
10.	3,345	MMMCCCXXXXV	MMMCCCXXXIIIII	MMMCCCXLV

The verb *can* is used to express mental or physical ability. *May* is used to express possibility or ask permission. The verb *lie* means to rest or recline. The verb *lay* means to put or place something. Circle the verb that correctly completes each sentence.

11. Bingo, (lie, lay) down!

12. Toto (may, can) do several tricks, such as sitting, shaking, and rolling over.

13. Mom, (may, can) Amy spend the night on Friday?

14. No one (may, can) understand the problem like Evelyn!

15. Janie (may, can) return to work when she is feeling well again.

16. If you see Melora, you (may, can) offer her a ride home.

17. Please (lie, lay) the paper on the stairs.

18. You may (lie, lay) the magazine on the table when you're finished looking at it.

19. I (may, can) reach the green only if I hit the ball a long way!

20. The cat wants to (lie, lay) down on the blanket.

DAY 20

Circle the mood of each sentence.

21. The grayish clouds overshadowed the day.
    A. happy
    B. sad
    C. quiet

22. Larry looked toward the ground and tried to hold back his tears.
    A. happy
    B. sad
    C. quiet

23. As the waves slowly touched the shore, the water whispered softly.
    A. happy
    B. sad
    C. quiet

24. The clown's bright costume jiggled as he played with the perky puppy.
    A. happy
    B. sad
    C. quiet

25. The children's laughter floated through the air as they splashed in the pool.
    A. happy
    B. sad
    C. quiet

26. A hushed silence fell over the crowd.
    A. happy
    B. sad
    C. quiet

Match each inventor with his invention. Use the Internet if you need help.

27. _____ Eli Whitney
28. _____ Elias Howe
29. _____ Levi Strauss
30. _____ Cyrus McCormick
31. _____ Samuel F. B. Morse
32. _____ Thomas Edison
33. _____ Alexander G. Bell

A. telegraph
B. phonograph
C. sewing machine
D. cotton gin
E. telephone
F. reaper
G. blue jeans

CHARACTER CHECK: Write down three good things that you are going to do today and do them!

How Do Lungs Work?

Have you ever wondered how your lungs are able to breathe in and out? In this activity, you will learn about how lungs work.

Materials

- balloons (2 small, 1 large)
- 2-liter plastic bottle
- masking tape
- rubber bands (small and large)
- 2 pipettes
- rubber tubing
- scissors

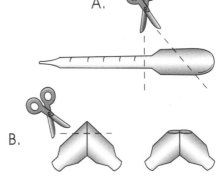

Procedure

1. Cut the pipettes (A). You may need an adult's help.
2. Place the pipette bulbs together and hold them together with tape. Then, cut off the tops of the bulbs, creating a "Y" connector (B).
3. Insert your new Y-shaped piece into the rubber tubing and tape it in place. Attach the two small balloons to the arms of the "Y" with small rubber bands.
4. Have an adult help you cut off the bottom of the 2-liter bottle.
5. Insert the tubing through the bottom of the bottle and out through the neck. Use tape to seal the tubing at the neck so that the balloons are suspended inside the bottle.
6. Cut the neck off the large balloon. Stretch the rest of the balloon over the bottom of the bottle. Use a large rubber band to keep it in place.
7. Pull on the bottom of the balloon, being careful not to pull it off the bottle. Watch what happens to the small balloons.

What's This All About?

The long tube at the top represents your trachea, where the air comes in. The two arms of the plastic piece represent bronchial tubes, which lead to the lungs. The small balloons are the lungs. By pulling on the bottom balloon, which represents the diaphragm (a large muscle under the lungs), you lower the pressure inside the bottle (your chest cavity). This causes the "lungs" to inflate because the outside air pressure is now higher than the inside air pressure and air rushes in to equalize it. When you let go of the diaphragm, you increase the inside air pressure and the lungs deflate as the air rushes out. The diaphragm (with help from other muscles) pulls air into the lungs and pushes it out again. While the air is inside, the lungs collect carbon dioxide from the blood and put oxygen back into it. The carbon dioxide is then pushed out with the next exhale.

* See page ii.

BONUS

All About Backbones

Where would you be without a backbone? You wouldn't be able to pick up your pencil if you dropped it. You wouldn't be able to walk. You wouldn't even be able to sit in a chair. Without a backbone, you wouldn't be able to do much of anything!

Materials
- 11 cardboard tubes (short)
- 11 rubber bands (1 inch long)
- hole punch
- scissors

Procedure
1. Cut each cardboard tube into thirds. If the tubes bend as you cut them, push them back to their original shapes.
2. Punch two holes on opposite sides of each tube section. Use the top illustration as a guide.
3. Loop the rubber bands together to form one long string. Thread the string of rubber bands through the holes in the tube sections one at a time. When all of the sections are threaded on the rubber-band string, tie off the string at the top and bottom.
4. Experiment by bending your handmade backbone in different directions. See if your backbone has limitations. Try to figure out what would happen if one or more sections were damaged or had to be removed.
5. Imagine that your real backbone is frozen into one solid piece for 60 seconds. Demonstrate how you would walk across the room, pick up a chair, and put it down again. Remember, none of your vertebrae can move for 60 seconds.

What's This All About?
The backbone serves as the major supporting structure in the body, so it must possess great rigidity. At the same time, it must be flexible enough to allow twisting, turning, and bending. To accommodate this movement, the backbone is divided into sections called vertebrae. The human body has 33 vertebrae. They permit swaying and bending and, at the same time, provide support for the head and places for the ribs to attach. Additionally, the delicate spinal cord runs through these vertebrae, with each vertebra providing openings or exit points where the spinal nerves can go to the various organs in the body.

Governing a Nation

The United States Constitution is organized into seven sections called articles. The articles are numbered with Roman numerals. Match each article with its summary. Use an encyclopedia, the Internet, or another reference if you need help.

1. _____ Article I

2. _____ Article II

3. _____ Article III

4. _____ Article IV

5. _____ Article V

6. _____ Article VI

7. _____ Article VII

A. says that at least nine states must accept the Constitution before it can become a law

B. states that the Constitution is the law of the land and that all senators and representatives must swear to support the Constitution

C. describes the powers of the Supreme Court and other federal courts

D. describes how the president will be elected, who can run for president, and what powers and responsibilities the president has

E. describes how the states will relate to each other, how new states can be added to the Union, and how the federal government will protect the states

F. describes how amendments, or changes, can be made to the Constitution

G. describes how Congress will be set up, how laws will be made, and what powers Congress will have

Read each description of Canada's system of government. Then, fill in the blanks to complete each description of the U.S. government.

8. Canada is comprised of 10 provinces and three territories. The United States is comprised of _____ states, the _____ of Columbia, and six territories.

9. Canada is a parliamentary democracy and a constitutional monarchy, with a king or queen of England as its head of state. The United States is a constitutional _____ with a _____ as its head of state.

10. Each province in Canada has its own legislature and is governed by a federally appointed commissioner. Each U.S. state has its own _____ and is governed by a _____ .

BONUS

United States Supreme Court

Read the passage. Then, circle *yes* or *no* to answer each question.

The U.S. Supreme Court is the highest court in the country. Its main job is to rule on cases that involve questions about laws in the Constitution. The Supreme Court also has the last say in cases that have gone through the lower courts. The Supreme Court is not like a trial court. Instead of one judge, there are nine, and there is no jury of U.S. citizens to make the decisions. The judges make the final decisions, called rulings. The Supreme Court cannot make new laws, but their rulings are similar to laws because all other courts must follow their decisions. The judges on the U.S. Supreme Court are called justices. Supreme Court justices are chosen by the president of the United States with approval from the Senate. After a judge is chosen as a Supreme Court justice, he or she has the job for life.

1. Can another court change the decision of a Supreme Court case?

   yes   no

2. Does the Supreme Court use a jury to make decisions?

   yes   no

3. Do other courts have to follow Supreme Court rulings?

   yes   no

4. Is there more than one judge on the Supreme Court?

   yes   no

5. Does the U.S. Senate choose the Supreme Court justices?

   yes   no

6. Does a Supreme Court justice lose his or her job after 10 years?

   yes   no

7. Can the Supreme Court write new laws?

   yes   no

8. Does the Supreme Court settle questions about the Constitution?

   yes   no

Research the current Supreme Court justices and write their names on a separate sheet of paper.

The States

Read the passage. Then, circle *true* or *false* for each statement.

From Alaska to Hawaii and California to Maine, the states of the United States have such different concerns that federal laws cannot meet each state's specific needs. State government allows each state to make rules and laws that are specific to its state. Each state has a capital city (like the country's capital, Washington, D.C.) where the government does its work. The organization of state government is similar to the organization of the federal government. Each state in the United States has an executive, a legislative, and a judicial branch of government. The executive branch in state government is headed by the state's governor. The legislative branch in all state governments except Nebraska has an upper house (usually called a senate) and a lower house (usually called a house of representatives) to make laws. (Nebraska has just one state house.) The judicial branch in state government contains state courts and a state supreme court. Each state also has its own constitution. One state's constitution and laws can be very different from another's but cannot go against the U.S. Constitution.

I.	Each state's constitution is the same.	true	false
2.	Each state has three branches of government.	true	false
3.	Every state has two houses in the legislative branch.	true	false
4.	Every state has a governor.	true	false
5.	A state's constitution can keep women from voting in that state.	true	false
6.	A governor is to a state as the president is to the country.	true	false
7.	State governments do their work in Washington, D.C.	true	false
8.	Federal laws are not specific enough to meet all states' needs.	true	false
9.	Each state has a supreme court.	true	false
10.	The executive branch makes the laws in state government.	true	false

Take It Outside!

Take a pen and a notebook and walk around your neighborhood. Pay special attention to street signs, house numbers, and building addresses. When you find a number, write it in your notebook. Make a list of all of the numbers you see. Then, rewrite all of the numbers as Roman numerals. Share the Roman numeral results with your friends and neighbors. Do they recognize the addresses written as Roman numerals?

Take a pen and a notebook outside and find a place to sit. Look around and observe what you see and hear. Identify something near where you are sitting, such as a tree, a bench, or a stream, that is a permanent feature. Imagine how this object might view the experiences of a typical day. Then, write a letter from the object's perspective to the people who pass by it every day.

With a family member, identify two parks in your community. Take a pen and a notebook and visit both parks. Make a list of what you find in each park. After your visits, review what is on your lists, noting what is on both lists and what appears on just one list. Next, use this information to create a Venn diagram that shows how the two parks are alike and how they are different.

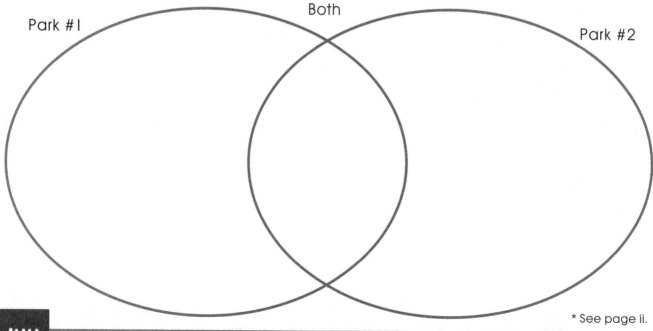

Park #1   Both   Park #2

* See page ii.

Section I

Day 1: 1. 21,411; 2. 84,525; 3. 892; 4. 519,549; 5. 1,212; 6. 661; 7. 42,094; 8. $1,668.41; 9. 71,130; 10. 12,848; Person: athlete, diver, manager, owner, senator; Place: canyon, courtyard, hilltop, mountain, valley; Thing: pillow, shoe, plate, napkin, ribbon; Idea: courage, joy, kindness, luck, trust; 11–20. Answers will vary. 21. E.; 22. D.; 23. B.; 24. H.; 25. G.; 26. F.; 27. C.; 28. A.

Day 2: 1. 2,685,322; 2. 910,478; 3. 23,409,036; 4. 1,342,111; 5. 405,234; 6. 16,053,245; 7. 30,000,000 + 7,000,000 + 100,000 + 20,000 + 6,000 + 400 + 80 + 9; 8. 50,000,000,000 + 6,000,000,000 + 400,000,000 + 80,000,000 + 7,000,000 + 300,000 + 20,000 + 900 + 60; 9. C; 10. C; 11. C; 12. C; 13. S; 14. P; 15. P; 16. S; 17. S; 18. P; 19. S; 20. S; 21. S; 22. C; 23. C; 24. P; 25. camping; 26. packed; 27. hunt; 28. picked; 29. Parking; 30. splashing; 31. Anchorage; 32. Los Angeles; 33. Kansas City; 34. New Orleans; 35. Detroit; 36. Ottawa; 37. Albuquerque; 38. New York City; 39. Columbus; 40. Calgary

Day 3: 1. 50 + 30 = 80; 2. 90 + 60 = 150; 3. 400 + 400 = 800; 4. 200 + 400 = 600; 5. 900 + 500 = 1,400; 6. 3,000 + 5,000 = 8,000; 7. 10,000 + 4,000 = 14,000; 8. 20,000 + 30,000 = 50,000; 9. 100,000 + 8,000 = 108,000; 10. 20,000 + 10,000 = 30,000; 11. reporters; 12. drivers; 13. driver's; 14. correct; 15. correct; 16. organizers; 17. The Lunar Module had landed on the moon.; 18. moon; 19. whether to remain in orbit or to descend to the lunar surface; 20. They were the first people to walk on the moon.; 21. Answers will vary.

Day 4: 1–10. Estimates will vary, but actual answers include: 1. 18,012; 2. 9,939; 3. 102,352; 4. 112,754; 5. 2,807; 6.1,229; 7. 46,406; 8. 55,563; 9. $167.16; 10. yes; 11. teachers'; 12. mountain; 13. deer; 14. geese, feet; 15. trout; 16. patients;

17. sheep; 18. scissors; 19–39. Answers will vary.

Day 5: 1–8. Estimates will vary, but actual answers include: 1. 12,770; 2. 12,726; 3. 286,157; 4. 588,349; 5. 12,792; 6. 51,675; 7. 6.8$\overline{3}$; 8. 3.575; 9. OP; 10. SP; 11. OP; 12. SP; 13. SP; 14. SP; 15. SP; 16. OP; 17. OP; 18. SP; 19. the act of punishing; 20. vanish; 21. to soak before; 22. to wind again; 23. without color; 24. cooked before; 25. not sure; 26. like brown

Day 6: 1. 432 cones (mult.); 2. 1,160 chocolates (add.); 3. 7,722 pounds (sub.); 4. $39.77 (add.); 5. I; 6. me; 7. I; 8. me; 9. Her; 10. his; 11. My; 12. mine; 13. C.; 14. an ecosystem; 15. Answers may include: grasslands, wetlands, tundra, mountain, maritime, temperate rain forests, temperate deciduous forests; 16. permafrost; 17. It is near the Atlantic Ocean.; 18. the Hudson Plains; 19. the sea

Day 7: 1. 28.875; 2. 661; 3. 1,237.8; 4. 98.5; 5. 9; 6. 1,846.175; 7. 99.$\overline{3}$; 8. 83.2; 9. his; 10. her; 11. my; 12. her; 13. their; 14. your; 15. an, a; 16. a; 17. an, a; 18. a, the, the; 19. a, a; 20. G.; 21. I.; 22. C.; 23. H.; 24. B.; 25. D.; 26. F.; 27. J.; 28. E.; 29. A.; 30. 45 years; 31. 27 years; 32. 18 years; 33. 48 years

Day 8: 1. 6 packages, ~~Each package costs $5.25.~~; 2. $1.25, ~~He also has a pet frog.~~; 3. 3 pints, ~~He is also baking 5 rolls in the oven.~~; Circled verbs include: walk, sound, call, dance, sit, caught, honked, smell, plays, wore, gather, throw, jump, won, dive, rolled, wiggled, sneezed, read, eat, cheer, meowing, barking, selling, climbs, skiing, paint, cry, built, speak, carried, bake, wash, practice, blew, clapped, watched, wants, mopped, hit, helped, carried, fed; Underlined verbs include: are, be, been, seem, being, will, were, is, am, become, have been, was, has, has had, became, have, had; 4. inlets; 5. stethoscope; 6. suspicious; 7. subscribe; 8. margin; 9. owes;

10. frank; 11. knead; 12. allergies; 13. conduct; Solids: box, dust, rock, ice; Liquids: juice, lava, milk, water; Gases: air, helium, hydrogen, oxygen

Day 9: 1. 70; 2. 160; 3. 920; 4. 800; 5. 2,500; 6. 4,200; 7. 100,000; 8. 4,500; 9. 4,200; 10. 12,000; 11. 60,000; 12. 240,000; 13. 8,000; 14. 27,000; 15. 150,000; 16. am; 17. is; 18. were; 19. was; 20. Are; 21. has been; 22. is being; 23. will be; 24–27. Answers will vary.; 28. North Carolina; 29. four years; 30. Answers will vary.; 31. C.

Day 10: 1. 38,822; 2. 16,936; 3. 15,687; 4. 49,623; 5. 172,072; 6. 288,357; 7. 90,741; 8. 457,666; 9. rang; 10. built; 11. fed; 12. chose; 13. spent; 14. spun; 15. ran; 16. awoke; 17. became; 18. brought; 19. drew; 20. grew; 21–35. Answers may be in any order: frostbite, bloodhound, playground, lifeguard, wristwatch, spacecraft, shipwreck, loudspeaker, clipboard, turtleneck, silverware, peppermint, headache, salesperson, viewpoint

Day 11: 1. 42; 2. 72; 3. 25; 4. 55; 5. 24; 6. 54; 7. 0; 8. 54; 9. 50; 10. 110; 11. 27; 12. 108; 13. 36; 14. 90; 15. 28; 16. 48; 17. 56; 18. 99; 19. 48; 20. 70; 21. 132; 22. 21; 23. 81; 24. 55; 25. 35; 26. 120; 27. 63; 28. 100; 29. 22; 30. 72; 31. 40; 32. 66; 33. 30; 34. 64; 35. 40; 36. 132; 37. ate; 38. shook; 39. held; 40. bled; 41. wrote; 42. rode; 43. taught; 44. fought; 45. froze; Proofreading marks should indicate: grandparents, sidewalk, outside, everyone, Whenever, someone, cowboys, football, suitcases, grandparents, everywhere, inside, railroad, newspaper, whatever, lighthouse, Nobody, lighthouse, anymore; 46. proprietor; 47. cash crops; 48. indigo; 49. indentured servants

Day 12: 1. 18; 2. 16; 3. 63; 4. 66; 5. 56; 6. 55; 7. 35; 8. 60; 9. 77; 10. 64; 11. 99; 12. 144; 13. 60; 14. 42; 15. 96; 16. 88; 17. 60; 18. 49; 19. 48; 20. 72; 21. 36; 22. 99; 23. 36; 24. 80; 25. Answers will include: fly, swim, ring, sing, see, begin, eat, go, bite; 26. Answers will include: flew, swam, rang, sang, saw, began, ate, went, bit; 27. Answers will include: flown, swum, rung, sung, seen, begun, eaten, gone, bitten; 28. remodel; 29. deposit; 30. giggle; 31. shelves; 32. penalty; 33. predict; 34. precise; 35. estimate; 36. business; 37. giant

Day 13: 1. 30; 2. 49; 3. 72; 4. 108; 5. 45; 6. 100; 7. 42; 8. 56; 9. 32; 10. 33; 11. 50; 12. 40; 13. 0; 14. 30; 15. 44; 16. 0; 17. 72; 18. 15; 19. 56; 20. 48; 21. 24; 22. 18; 23. 144; 24. 88; 25. 20; 26. 60; 27. 63; 28. 132; 29. 36; 30. 0; 31. 77; 32. 70; 33. 72; 34. 90; 35. 20; 36. 88; 37. will build; 38. will check; 39. will map; 40. will board; 41. will count; 42. will launch; 43. will view; 44. will observe; 45. will record; 46. will photograph; 47. 4; 48. Precambrian, Paleozoic, Mesozoic, Cenozoic; 49. Mesozoic; 50. 3; 51. Triassic, Jurassic, Cretaceous; 52. Cenozoic

Day 14: 1. jumbo; 2. 6 dozen small eggs; 3. large; 4. 72, small; 5. 120 ounces; 6. should not; 7. they will; 8. I have; 9. you are; 10. what is/what has; 11. wasn't; 12. he's; 13. she'll; 14. they'd; 15. you've; ~~Febuary~~ February, ~~Journel~~ Journal, ~~definately~~ definitely, ~~calender~~ calendar, ~~naybor~~ neighbor, ~~suprised~~ surprised, ~~cuboards~~ cupboards, ~~vacume~~ vacuum, ~~your~~ you're, ~~especialy~~ especially, ~~priviledge~~ privilege, ~~untill~~ until

Day 15: 1–8. Answers will vary but may include: 1. 5, 10, 15, 20, 25; 2. 18, 27, 36, 45, 54; 3. 20, 30, 40, 50, 60; 4. 24, 36, 48, 60, 72; 5. 12, 24, 36; 6. 10, 20, 30; 7. 28, 56, 84; 8. 24, 48, 72; 9. 18; 10. 12; 11. 30; 12. 40; 13–27. Answers will vary.

Day 16: 1. ⁻5, ⁻4, ⁻3, ⁻2, ⁻1; 2–6. Students should circle the words in green: 2. <u>wild</u>, <u>eerie</u>, **wind**; 3. <u>fuzzy</u>, <u>brown</u>, **caterpillar**; 4. <u>fresh</u>, <u>cool</u>, **water**; 5. <u>hot</u>, <u>tired</u>, **explorers**; <u>large</u>, <u>clear</u>, **lake**; 6. <u>spicy</u>, **aroma**; <u>apple</u>,

cider; <u>Jason's</u>, <u>small</u>, <u>warm</u>, **tent**; 7. longest; 8. wider; 9. youngest; 10. largest; 11. smaller; 12. C.; 13. light, water, carbon dioxide; 14. chlorophyll; 15. a type of sugar; 16. They keep a balance between oxygen and carbon dioxide.

Day 17: 1. 9; 2. 0; 3. -8; 4. 4; 5. -2; 6. <; 7. >; 8. >; 9. <; 10. >; 11. >; 12. PA; 13. PN; 14. PA; 15. PN; 16. PA; 17. PA; 18. PN; 19. PA; 20. PA, PA; **Across:** 2. smart, 3. great, 4. chew, 5. remember, 6. doctor, **Down:** 1. wellknown (well-known), 2. starving, 3. grabbed, 4. crowd; 2, 1, 5, 6, 7, 4, 3

Day 18: 1. $\frac{3}{6}$ or $\frac{1}{2}$; 2. $\frac{3}{4}$; 3. $\frac{5}{8}$; 4. $\frac{2}{3}$; 5. $\frac{3}{7}$; 6. $\frac{7}{12}$; 7. $\frac{5}{6}$; 8. $\frac{5}{16}$; 9–11. Order of answers may vary. 9. immediately, lately, never, often, soon, today; 10. carefully, eagerly, hard, quickly, softly, widely; 11. above, far, here, inside, there, upstairs; 12. moist; 13. enclosed; 14. ignorant; 15. freeze; 16. valuable; 17. outer core, inner core; 18. mantle; 19. lithosphere; 20. core; 21. center of the Earth

Day 19: 1–5. Order of fractions on number line: $\frac{1}{12}$, $\frac{3}{12}$, $\frac{5}{12}$, $\frac{7}{12}$, $\frac{10}{12}$; 6. <; 7. =; 8. >; 9. <; 10. =; 11. =; 12. <; 13. <; 14. =; 15. is healing, <u>nicely</u>; 16. moved, <u>rapidly</u>; 17. sang, <u>well</u>; 18. waited, <u>eagerly</u>; 19. chattered, <u>noisily</u>; 20–24. Answers will vary.; 25. A.; 26. Answers may include: Olympic Games, democracy, statues, buildings, medical texts, trade routes, epic poetry; 27. Modern sports arenas are based on ancient Greek stadiums.; 28. more than 1,000 years; 29. Their medical texts were used for hundreds of years.

Day 20: 1. 6; 2. 10; 3. 5; 4. 16; 5. 48; 6. 12; 7. 15; 8. 21; 9. 48; 10. 15; 11. 60; 12. 9; 13. 45; 14. 20; 15. 15; 16. 96; 17. more quietly, most quietly; 18. more smoothly, most smoothly;

19. more frequently, most frequently; 20. more clearly, most clearly; 21. more closely, most closely; 22. more patiently, most patiently; 23. sooner, soonest; 24. more roughly, most roughly; 25. more neatly, most neatly; 26. faster, fastest; 27. enjoys; 28. destroy; 29. often; 30. foolish; 31. reality; 32–34. Answers will vary.

U.S. States and Capitals: 1. s.; 2. F.; 3. i.; 4. J.; 5. q.; 6. L.; 7. c.; 8. H.; 9. x.; 10. X.; 11. b.; 12. S.; 13. h.; 14. K.; 15. j.; 16. P.; 17. r.; 18. W.; 19. t.; 20. D.; 21. o.; 22. B.; 23. g.; 24. U.; 25. y.; 26. N.; 27. d.; 28. I.; 29. w.; 30. R.; 31. m.; 32. T.; 33. u.; 34. C.; 35. e.; 36. M.; 37. n.; 38. G.; 39. k.; 40. V.; 41. p.; 42. E.; 43. v.; 44. A.; 45. a.; 46. Q.; 47. l.; 48. Y.; 49. f.; 50. O.

Section II

Day 1: 1. $\frac{28}{3}$; 2. $\frac{7}{2}$; 3. $\frac{19}{4}$; 4. $\frac{13}{2}$; 5. $\frac{9}{2}$; 6. 7; 7. $\frac{7}{3}$; 8. $\frac{5}{4}$; 9. 4; 10. 8; 11. 16; 12. 36; 13–21. Students should circle the words in orange: 13. **put**, <u>money</u>; 14. **bought**, <u>groceries</u>; 15. **begged**, <u>musicians</u>; 16. **found**, <u>coins</u>; 17. **melted**, <u>icicles</u>; 18. **made**, <u>touchdown</u>; 19. **loaded**, <u>furniture</u>; 20. **sold**, <u>tickets</u>; 21. **ruined**, <u>kite</u>; 22–31. Answers will vary.; 32. It has a magnetic field; 33. The north and south poles; 34. by studying the magnetic particles within rocks

Day 2: 1–10. Pictures will vary, but actual answers include: 1. $\frac{3}{8}$; 2. $\frac{1}{8}$; 3. $\frac{1}{6}$; 4. $\frac{2}{9}$; 5. $\frac{1}{9}$; 6. $\frac{1}{12}$; 7. $\frac{8}{15}$; 8. $\frac{4}{9}$; 9. $\frac{1}{6}$; 10. $\frac{3}{10}$; 11–20. Students should circle the words in orange: 11. <u>gave</u>, **puppy**, <u>bath</u>; 12. <u>wished</u>, **grandmother**, <u>birthday</u>; 13. <u>gave</u>, **Alan**, <u>swing</u>; 14. <u>handed</u>, **Kent**, <u>platter</u>; 15. <u>offered</u>, **Tommy**, <u>pencil</u>; 16. <u>knitted</u>, **Davetta**, <u>scarf</u>; 17. <u>gave</u>, **cat**, <u>treat</u>; 18. <u>wrote</u>, **pen pals**, <u>letters</u>; 19. <u>made</u>, **family**, <u>stir-fry</u>; 20. <u>saved</u>, **Rico**, <u>corn</u>; 21. C.; 22. about 3,500 years (from 2600 BC to AD 900);

23. Guatemala, Belize, El Salvador, parts of Honduras and southeast Mexico; 24. watch the movement of the planets and stars; 25. It had 260 days with a festival every 20th day.

Day 3: 1. $\frac{3}{10}$; 2. $\frac{4}{9}$; 3. $\frac{3}{16}$; 4. $\frac{10}{21}$; 5. $\frac{8}{35}$; 6. $\frac{1}{18}$; 7. $\frac{5}{36}$; 8. $\frac{1}{7}$; 9. $\frac{1}{4}$; 10. $\frac{2}{9}$; 11–18. Answers will vary.; 19. chews; 20. cheap; 21. bear; 22. pale; 23. manor; 24. tiers; 25. pole; 26. lesson; 27. 16; 28. Boston Massacre, Boston Tea Party; 29. the Stamp Act, 9 years; 30. King George III; 31. Lexington and Concord

Day 4: 1. C.; 2. F.; 3. A.; 4. E.; 5. B.; 6. D.; 7. $\frac{2}{9}$; 8. $\frac{15}{7}$; 9. $\frac{82}{7}$, 7, 5, 11$\frac{5}{7}$; 10. improper, 5$\frac{3}{5}$, 1$\frac{5}{12}$, 8$\frac{3}{7}$; 11–14. underline; 15–17. no underline; 18. underline; 19–20. no underline; 21–22. underline; 23–25. no underline; 26. knew, new; 27. hour, our; 28. read; 29. buy, to; 30. their; 31. two; 32. see, sea; 33. tail

Day 5: 1. $\frac{15}{8}$; 2. $\frac{3}{2}$; 3. $\frac{2}{3}$; 4. 2; 5. $\frac{6}{5}$; 6. $\frac{1}{3}$; 7. $\frac{9}{7}$; 8. $\frac{2}{5}$; 9. $\frac{15}{16}$; 10. $\frac{21}{4}$; 11. $\frac{7}{3}$; 12. $\frac{10}{9}$; 13. and; 14. but; 15. and; 16. or; 17. and; 18. but; 19. but; 20. and; 21. C.; 22. 4, 1, 3, 2; 23. She led American soldiers on a raid.; 24. Answers may include: helped the freed slaves, cared for the elderly, worked for women's rights

Day 6: 1. 30.41; 2. 24.683; 3. 9.096; 4. 19.14; 5. 451.606; 6. 342.325; 7. 51.841; 8. $107.02; 9–15. Answers will vary.; 16. be, bee; 17. Aunt, ant; 18. band, banned; 19. I'll, Isle; 20. close, clothes; 21. sent, cent; 22. blue, blew; 23. by, buy; 24. ate, eight; 25. No, know

Day 7:

Date	Deposited	Withdrew	Total $
May 15	$500.25	$0	$500.25
May 31	$496.80	$0	$997.05
June 4	$0	$145.00	$852.05
June 15	$435.20	$0	$1,287.25
June 30	$600.00	$0	$1,887.25
July 1	$0	$463.00	$1,424.25
July 15	$110.00	$0	$1,534.25
July 24	$0	$600.00	$934.25

1. $934.25; 2. Folklore is passed from generation to generation.; 3. The early cattle ranchers drove their cattle to the market.; 4. Nassim rides his bike to school most days.; 5. The snake in the science corner escaped from its cage.; 6. Can you balance a book on your head?; 7. S; 8. F; 9. F; 10. S; 11–19. Answers will vary but may include: 11. mouth; 12. soup; 13. painting; 14. addresses; 15. gardener; 16. afternoon; 17. reasonable; 18. ad(vertisement); 19. school; 20–28. Answers will vary but may include: 20. mine, mines, seem, seen; 21. larva, crab, oral, vocal; 22. pint, spot, pots, script; 23. pose, pops, pups, spur; 24. pens, pend, ends, ended; 25. exam, mine, miner, rime; 26. plume, mule, pled, lump; 27. soil, Sioux, soul, sour; 28. noon, soot, moon, mount

Day 8: 1. 7.055; 2. 0.7412; 3. 259.86; 4. 0.0117; 5. 0.518; 6. 0.207; 7. 0.0007; 8. 0.275; 9. S; 10. F; 11. R; 12. F; 13. S; 14. S; 15. S; 16. R; 17. A.; 18. life science; 19. plants, animals, bacteria, ecosystems; 20. a community in which plants and animals live together; 21. It can affect all other parts.; 22. Answers will vary.

Day 9: 1. 0.72; 2. 0.56; 3. 13.8; 4. 40.4; 5. 84.5; 6. 53.368; 7. 365.1232; 8. 512.05; 9. 498.852; 10. 2,514.255; 11. D (.); 12. In (?); 13. D (.); 14. Im (.); 15. In (?); 16. D (.); 17. In (?); 18. D (.); 19. E (!); 20. In (?); 21. E (!); 22. Im (.); 23. hand; 24. states; 25. foot; 26. go; 27. vine; 28. dog; 29. street (road); 30. den; 31. sculpture

Day 10: 1. 1.8; 2. 2.6; 3. 3.7; 4. 4.6; 5. 89; 6. 23.6; 7. 45.9; 8. 78.5; 9. 69.1; 10. 55.5; 11–20. Answers will vary.; 21–25. Answers will vary but may include: 21. She had a pleasant voice.; 22. The cat has smooth fur.; 23. The water is shiny and blue.; 24. Kristen absorbed the information.; 25. He stood straight.; 26. Answers will vary.; earthquake, energy, fault, fracture, focus, above, epicenter, beneath, Seismic waves, Seismologists

Day 11: 1. 131.66; 2. 215.50; 3. 106,603; 4. 15,792; 5. 264,208; 6. 4,202,534; 7. 1,328.25; 8. 9,875.5; 9. $\frac{33}{4}$; 10. $\frac{21}{2}$; 11. $\frac{183}{20}$; 12. $\frac{21}{4}$; 13. <u>owl</u>, <u>watches</u>; 14. <u>Worms</u>, <u>burrow</u>; 15. <u>orca</u>, <u>surfaces</u>; 16. <u>Moths</u>, <u>flutter</u>; 17. <u>elephant</u>, <u>trumpets</u>; 18. <u>spider</u>, <u>captures</u>; 19. <u>gazelles</u>, <u>stampede</u>; 20. <u>Koalas</u>, <u>climb</u>; 21. <u>hawk</u>, <u>scans</u>; 22. <u>fox</u>, <u>slinks</u>; 23. C.; 24. funding a new park, changing a law; 25. No one can see how you vote.; 26. by pulling levers to select their candidates; 27. by punch cards or on computers

Day 12: 1–8. Order of answers may vary: 1. 56 x 39 = 2,184; 2,184 ÷ 39 = 56; 2,184 ÷ 56 = 39; 2. 37 x 95 = 3,515; 3,515 ÷ 37 = 95; 3,515 ÷ 95 = 37; 3. 76 x 49 = 3,724; 3,724 ÷ 76 = 49; 3,724 ÷ 49 = 76; 4. 27 x 151 = 4,077; 4,077 ÷ 27 = 151; 4,077 ÷ 151 = 27; 5. 3,762 ÷ 99 = 38; 99 x 38 = 3,762; 38 x 99 = 3,762; 6. 26,320 ÷ 560 = 47; 47 x 560 = 26,320; 560 x 47 = 26,320; 7. 48,306 ÷ 582 = 83; 83 x 582 = 48,306; 582 x 83 = 48,306; 8. 92 x 194 = 17,848; 17,848 ÷ 92 = 194; 17,848 ÷ 194 = 92; 9–17. Students should circle the words in orange: 9. A giant **tortoise**; 10. Baby **pandas**; 11. An alligator's **eye**; 12. **Giraffes**; 13. **lives** in a nest high in an old elm tree; 14. **awakens** in his leafy nest late in the morning; 15. **left** early in the morning; 16. **races** along the elm's branches; 17. **scampers** down the tree trunk; 18. midnight; 19. mouse; 20. shiny; 21. flat; 22. swings; 23. rocket

Day 13: 1. 2:30; 2. 8:15; 3. 6:30; 4. 3:00; 5. 8:10 A.M.; 6. 10:50 P.M.; 7–14. Students should circle each word in orange: 7. **Carmen** ~~walks~~ carefully along the rocky shore.; 8. **Pools** of water ~~collect~~ in rocky crevices near the shore.; 9. **Tide pools** ~~are~~ home to sea plants and animals.; 10. **Seaweed** ~~is~~ the most common tide pool plant.; 11. **They** ~~provide~~ food and shelter for a variety of animals.; 12. **Carmen** ~~sees~~ spiny sea urchins attached to a rock.; 13. Their **mouths** ~~are~~ on their undersides.; 14. Their sharp **teeth** ~~cut~~ seaweed into little pieces.; 15–19. Answers will vary.

Day 14: 1. 128; 2. 14; 3. 19; 4. 26; 5. 30; 6. 26; 7. 126; 8. 26; 9–16. Students should circle the words in orange: 9. CP, **planted, raised**; 10. CS, **Chinese, Japanese**; 11. N; 12. CS, **Fish, shellfish**; 13. CS, **Overfishing, pollution**; 14. CS, **Sea farming, ranching**; 15. CP **raise, sell**; 16. CP, **grow, taste**; 17. C.; 18. land and other resources; 19. They were forced to move if settlers wanted their land.; 20. lands farther west (Oklahoma); 21. the long journey west that the Cherokees were forced to make

Day 15: 1. 20; 2. 10; 3. 19; 4. 36; 5. 10; 6. 4; 7. 6; 8. 2; 9. 13; 10. 13; 11–20. Students should circle the words in orange: 11. **bivalve** → mussel, <u>is</u>; 12. **sister** → girl, <u>is</u>; 13. **teacher** → Mrs. Stamey, <u>is</u>; 14. **student** → I, <u>am</u>; 15. **tool** → calculator, <u>is</u>; 16. **ball** → Jupiter, <u>is</u>; 17. **planet** → Venus, <u>is</u>; 18. **Marcus Bolan** → player, <u>is</u>; 19. **star** → sun, <u>is</u>; 20. **afghan** → yarn, <u>will be</u>; 21. S, trees, soldiers; 22. S, cars, ants; 23. M, sound, dogs; 24. S, clowns, sardines; 25. M, feet, drums; 26. lines indicate darkest areas; 27. because one plate is pushed against another

Day 16: 1. 9; 2. 5; 3. 26; 4. 89; 5. 877; 6. 657; 7. 200; 8. 1,395; 9. 5,529; 10. 40; 11. 47,127; 12. 190,498; 13–22. Students should circle the

words in orange: 13. **disgusting** → Ants, <u>are</u>; 14. **delicious** → hamburgers, <u>are</u>; 15. **unvarnished** → deck, <u>was</u>; 16. **great** → abilities, <u>are</u>; 17. **beautiful** → cake, <u>is</u>; 18. **sizeable** → dent, <u>was</u>; 19. **better** → Terrance, <u>will feel</u>; 20. **sore** → back, <u>was</u>; 21. **ecstatic** → Mrs. Tribble, <u>was</u>; 22. **happy** → Wendy, I, <u>were</u>; 23. M; 24. S; 25. M; 26. M; 27. S; 28. Life, Liberty, and the pursuit of Happiness; 29. to secure the basic rights of people; 30. to alter it or abolish it and institute new Government

Day 17: 1. N: 95, 40; 2. M: 73, N: 68; 3. M: 70, N: 64, Rule: M – 9 = N; 4. M: 30, N: 13, Rule: M – 11 = N; 5. N: 60, 36, Rule: M × 6 = N; 6. N: 6, 4, Rule: M ÷ 3 = N; 7. M: 9, 6, Rule: M × 9 = N; 8. M: 12, 11, Rule: M × 12 = N; 9–16. Students should circle words in orange: 9. <u>is walking</u>; 10. <u>has shopped</u>; 11. **<u>might have</u>** called, **had** known; 12. <u>is closed</u>; 13. **does** enjoy; 14. <u>is playing</u>; 15. **does** finish; 16. **are** watching; 17. B.; 18. World War II; 19. block proposals brought to the council by voting against them; 20. 5 years; 21. Answers may include: provides peacekeepers; helps victims of natural disasters; promotes workers' rights; provides food, medicine, and safe drinking water for those in need

Day 18: 1. G.; 2. F.; 3. B.; 4. E.; 5. A.; 6. I.; 7. H.; 8. C.; 9. D.; 10. The frogs sleep during the day, and they hunt for food at night.; 11. A parrot's bright colors are easy to see in a tree, but a tree boa's green color makes it difficult to spot.; 12. A fruit bat has a long nose, and it has large eyes to see in the dark.; 13. I know math well.; 14. Who told the secret?; 15. He is just like his father.; 16. She will sleep very well tonight.; 17. The two friends are very similar.; 18. T; 19. T; 20. F; 21. F; 22. F; 23. T; 24. T; 25. F; 26. T

Day 19: 1–9. Answers will vary.; 10–16. Students should draw three lines under letters in orange:

10. Automobiles; 11. **I**; 12. Yes; 13. Erupting; 14. **Weather**; 15. Britain's; 16. **Trees**; 17. C.; 18. C.; 19. A.; 20. A.; 21. B.; 22. A.

Day 20: 1. 46; 2. 24; 3. 21; 4. 110; 5. 80; 6. 124; 7. Cousin Sylvia; 8. Uncle Vernon; 9. Jerry Andrews; 10. Aunt Martha; 11. Paulo Joe Rollo; 12. Grandfather Murray; 13. Mr. and Mrs. Foster; 14. Dr. C. L. Smith; 15. Ms. Maxine Marshall; 16. Miss Tiffany Tyler; 17. C.; 18. to help predict future weather; 19. Answers may include: temperature, wind speed, atmospheric pressure, precipitation; 20. They can predict how climate and weather might change in the future.; 21. when it might strike and how to stay safe

The Mayflower Compact: 1. opinion; 2. fact; 3. opinion; 4. fact; 5. opinion; 6. fact; 7. fact; 8. opinion

The Branches of the U.S. Government: 1. legislative; 2. legislative; 3. executive; 4. judicial; 5. executive; Pie chart will vary but may include: The executive branch carries out federal laws, recommends new laws, directs national defense and foreign policy, appoints justices, and performs ceremonial duties.; The legislative branch makes laws, passes laws, impeaches officials, and approves treaties.; The judicial branch interprets the Constitution, reviews laws, and decides cases involving states' rights.

Reading Rainfall Maps: 1. Hawaii; 2. more than 200 inches; 3. less than 8 inches; 4. more than 200 inches; 5. Kamuela; 6. Flagstaff; 7. Tucson, Phoenix; 8. Honokaa, Kailua-Kona

Section III

Day 1: 1. 20; 2. 64; 3. 432; 4. 12; 5. 104; 6. 840; Industrial Revolution, Her, Great Depression, Governor, Mayor, Immigrant's, English, French, German, Scandinavian, Italian, Father, Spartans, Mars; 7. alleys; 8. deciding; 9. enemy; 10. hurried;

11. identify; 12. individual; 13. journey;
14. reunite; 15. subscription; 16. toil;
17. toiletry; 18. victorious; 19. A.;
20. American Northwest

Day 2: 1. 69.08 inches; 2. 9 cm,
56.52 cm; 3. 20 meters, 62.8 meters;
4. 26 yards, 81.64 yards; 5. 24 feet,
48 feet; 6. 21 inches, 131.88 inches;
7. 34 cm, 106.76 cm; 8. 45 mm,
90 mm; 9. 50 inches, 100 inches;
10. ?; 11. ?; 12. ?; 13. !; 14. !; 15. ?;
16. !; 17. ?; 18–19. Answers will vary.;
20. dramatize, dra-mə-tīz ; 21. 3;
22. to behave dramatically;
23–24. Answers will vary.

Day 3: 1. angle; 2. vertex; 3. degree;
4. protractor; 5. 180; 6. right; 7. 90;
8. acute; 9. obtuse; 10. acute;
11. right; 12. obtuse; 13. Edmond,
Alberta; 14. North Branch, New York;
15. Dear Grandma,; 16. Dear Uncle
Gerald,; 17. Yours truly,; 18. March
3, 2010; 19. October 9, 2015; 20. Fall
Leaf, KS; 21. C.; 22. to buy stamps,
and mail letters and packages;
23. on foot, by car, by truck, or by
airplane; 24. a country's national
post office; 25. the size and weight
of an item, the distance to its
destination, and its target delivery
date

Day 4: 1. 25°; 2. 90°; 3. 20°; 4. 150°;
5–7. Check student's work.; 8. no;
9. no; 10. yes; 11. Commas are
inserted after: Debbie, Don,;
12. business, cultural,; 13. Bronx,
Manhattan, Queens, Brooklyn,;
14. Chinatown, Greenwich Village,;
15. Square, Center,; 16. no; 17. yes;
18. yes; 19. no; 20. no; 21. yes; 22. yes;
23. yes; 24. yes; 25. no; 26. yes;
27. yes; 28. no; 29. yes; 30. no

Day 5: 1. 60 m³; 2. 160 in.³;
3. 41.354 m³; 4. 240 mm³; 5. 38.4
in.³; 6. 384 cm³; 7. "What are the
rules for this game?"; 8. "Please set
the table,"; 9. "What's that terrible
noise?"; 10. "Tennessee Waltz";
11. "I don't think that I can do
this by myself,"; 12. "America the
Beautiful"; 13. "Do you like baseball

or football better?" Debra asked. "I
like baseball best."; 14. "Not me,"
answered Eleanor. "I like basketball
best."; 15. horse; 16. music; 17. home;
18. story; 19. young tree; 20. clothing;
21. 63; 22. 28; 23. 56; 24. 52.$\overline{3}$

Day 6: 1. congruent; 2. congruent;
3. similar; 4. similar; 5. congruent;
6. similar; 7. eighty-seven; 8. thirty-
nine; 9. forty-three; 10. one-half;
11. nine-tenths; 12. three-fourths;
13. two hundred ninety-two;
14. seven hundred eighty-one;
15. C.; 16. for religious freedom or
for more land for their families;
17. horses, oxen, and sheep;
18. in one-room schoolhouses
or at home; 19. doctor's office,
blacksmith's shop, general store

Day 7: 1. 1; 2. 1.5 or $1\frac{1}{2}$; 3. 24; 4.
4; 5. 2; 6. 21; 7. 36; 8. 3; 9. 9; 10. 0.5
or $\frac{1}{2}$; 11. 30; 12. 132; 13. use; 14.
propels; 15. are; 16. dig; 17. carries;
18. enjoy; 19. steers; 20. is; 21–23.
Answers will vary but may include:
21. The Table of Contents is arranged
by chapters. The Index is arranged
alphabetically by subject.; 22. in the
Index; 23. in the Table of Contents,
Chapter Six, page 260; 24. 5; 25. 172

Day 8: 1. 250; 2. 3,000; 3. 900;
4. 1,000; 5. 12,000; 6. 800; 7. 5;
8. 10,000; 9. 400,000; work, selects,
go, like, choose, take, grab, sit,
have, finish, share, meet, explains,
answers, enjoy; 10. Timbuktu is a
small trading town in central Mali.;
11. It was a trading post for products
from North and West Africa.; 12. It is
not as important or populated as it
once was.

Day 9: 1. 2; 2. 48; 3. 0.5 or $\frac{1}{2}$; 4. 0.25 or
$\frac{1}{4}$; 5. 2,000; 6. 2; 7. 1; 8. 6; 9. 1; 10. 1; 11.
1; 12. 0.625 or $\frac{1}{16}$; Answers will vary but

may include:
1624 Bay Lane
Short Creek, PA 12525
May 10, 2009

Dear Aunt Ann and Uncle James,

School will soon be out for the
summer. I am looking forward to it. The
year was good, and I learned a lot.

Mom and Dad are going to France
in July. I don't want to go with them. I'm
writing this letter to ask if I can stay with
you July 10 through July 22. I would love
to help you take care of the horses and
do anything else that you would want
me to do. I would also help around the
house. Please let me know if I can come.

Your loving niece,
Julie Ann

13. 3, 1, 2, 4; 14. Pulitzer Prize;
15. people who lived in the part of
Chicago where she lived; 16. C.

Day 10: 1. 1; 2. 1; 3. 4,000; 4. 5,000;
5. 3; 6. 9,000; 7. 8,000; 8. 4; 9. 9,500;
10. 2,000,000; 11. 9; 12. 7,000,000;

Juan Roberts
1624 Bay Lane
Short Creek, PA 12526

Mr. Barry York and Mrs. Melinda York
1010 Sunset Ranch Rd.
Ely, ID 89621

13–14. Answers will vary.; 15. heating
and pressure; 16. melting and
crystallization; 17. sedimentation
and compaction; 18. heating
and pressure; 19. melting and
crystallization; 20. sedimentation
and compaction

Day 11: 1. 20%; 2. 50%; 3. 8%; 4. 47%;
5. 9%; 6. $\frac{19}{100}$; 7. $\frac{24}{100}$; 8. $\frac{87}{100}$; 9. $\frac{36}{100}$;
10. $\frac{99}{100}$; 11. $\frac{1}{2}$; 12. $\frac{9}{10}$; 13. $\frac{1}{5}$; 14. $\frac{9}{20}$;
15. $\frac{7}{10}$; 16. read; 17. grew; 18. began;
19. held; 20. won; 21. led; 22. left;
23. went; 24–28. Answers will vary but
may include: 24. pretended;
25. coworkers; 26. on time; 27. stamp
collector; 28. rouse; 3, 1, 2, 4

Day 12: 1. 80%, 0.8; 2. 25%, 0.25;
3. 47%, 0.47; 4. 0.27; 5. 0.35; 6. 0.54;
7. 0.43; 8. 15%; 9. 88%; 10. 7%; 11. 91%;
12. regions; 13. grip; 14. primates;

15. termites; 16. pokes; 17. plucks; 18. charge, ripping; 19. bounds; 20. A.; 21. Earth's materials and structure; 22. movement of plates on Earth's crust, volcanoes, earthquakes, movement of glaciers; 23. to help plants grow better; 24. interpret data

Day 13: 1. Country; 2. Jazz; 3. 175; 4. 157.14285; 5. Answers will vary.; 6. gigantic; 7. ornately; 8. audience; 9. thirty-year-old; 10. enormous; 11. completely; 12. magnificently; 13. brilliantly; 14. enthusiastically; 15. splendid; 16. sluggish and lazy (dashes); 17. flat-bladed ax (phrase); 18. highly-seasoned stew (commas); 19. kneecap (phrase); 20. xylophone (parentheses)

Day 14: 1. $2.50; 2. $4.00; 3. $5.00; 4. $6.00; 5–10. Answers will vary but may include: 5. The team didn't want any trouble.; 6. Haven't you ever seen Yellowstone National Park?; 7. There aren't any eggs in the carton.; 8. He wasn't near any base when he was tagged out.; 9. There isn't any way to get there from here.; 10. The explanation didn't make any sense.; 11. C.; 12. B.; 13. A.; 14. B.; 15. D.; 16. C.; 17. A.; 18. E.

Day 15: 1. Monday; 2. 10 family members; 3. 250; 4. Wednesday; 5. 55; 6. Answers will vary; 7–11. Answers will vary but may include: 7. Can't anyone solve the puzzle?; 8. Rick didn't have anything to read.; 9. Annie had never seen that.; 10. Don't spill any of the juice.; 11. There isn't anything you can do about it.; 12. A.; 13. 2, 4, 1, 3; 14. New Orleans; 15. admiral

Day 16: 1. 16; **Today,** the term "American Indian" is used to describe people indigenous to **America. However,** the **first** explorers who came to America referred to them as **"Indians." Unknown** to the explorers, most tribes had their own names. **For example,** the name used by the **Delaware Indians** of eastern

North America meant "genuine men." **The** Indians' **languages,** ways of life, and homes **were** all very different. The **Aztec** and **Maya** Indians of **Central America** built large **cities.** The **Apache** and Paiute used brushes and **matting** to make simple **huts. The Plains Indians built cone-shaped** tepees covered with buffalo **skins.** Cliff **Dwellers** and other Pueblo groups **used** sun-dried bricks to make many-**storied houses.** 2–5. Answers will vary but may include: 2. so, snow, white ground; 3. so, electricity went out, went out to dinner; 4. so, unlatched gate, cattle were in the road; 5. so, Scott had the flu, he had to miss school; 6. D.; 7. B.; 8. C.; 9. A.

Day 17: 1. 50% or $\frac{1}{2}$; 2. 12.5% or $\frac{1}{8}$; 3. 25% or $\frac{1}{4}$; 4. 12.5% or $\frac{1}{8}$; 5. $\frac{2}{11}$; 6. $\frac{1}{11}$; 7. $\frac{1}{11}$; 8. $\frac{0}{11}$; 9. $\frac{3}{11}$; 10. $\frac{1}{11}$; 11–14. Answers will vary but may include: 11. Jim, Sean, and Maria liked to visit Grandma and Grandpa.; 12. Grandpa had horses, cows, and goats on his farm.; 13. Grandma raised chickens, ducks, and geese.; 14. Daisies, tulips, and roses grew in her garden.; 15–24. Answers will vary.

Day 18: 1. (multiples of 4) 4, 8, 12, 16; (multiples of 4 and 5) 0, 20; (multiples of 5) 5, 10, 15, 25; 2.

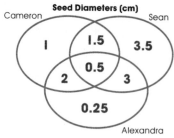

Seed Diameters (cm)

3. Walter; 4. Gerald; 5. Alejandro; 6. Ian; 7. Dad; 8. Betsy; 9. Donna; 10. Tara; 11. C.; 12. Massachusetts, Rhode Island, New Hampshire, Connecticut, Maine, Vermont; 13. to find religious freedom;

14. fishing and trading; 15. beautiful autumn foliage, fishing industry

Day 19: 1–4.

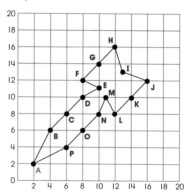

5. Who; 6. Whom; 7. Who; 8. Who; 9. Who; 10. Who; 11. Whom; 12. who; 13. whom; 14. whom; 15. trophy, proudly stood; 16. clouds, spit icicles; 17. leaves, sing, danced; 18. Horns, angrily; 19. sun, played hide-and-seek

Day 20: 1. CCCLXV; 2. MMIII; 3. DCCXCVI; 4. DCCCXLVII; 5. MDCCXLII; 6. MMMCDXCI; 7. DCCCLXV; 8. MDCCCXXXVIII; 9. MMCCCXLV; 10. MMMCCCXLV; 11. lie; 12. can; 13. may; 14. can; 15. may; 16. may; 17. lay; 18. lay; 19. can; 20. lie; 21. B.; 22. B.; 23. C.; 24. A.; 25. A.; 26. C.; 27. D.; 28. C.; 29. G.; 30. F.; 31. A.; 32. B.; 33. E.

Governing a Nation: 1. G.; 2. D.; 3. C.; 4. E.; 5. F.; 6. B.; 7. A.; 8. 50, District; 9. democracy, president; 10. legislature, governor

United States Supreme Court: 1. no; 2. no; 3. yes; 4. yes; 5. no; 6. no; 7. no; 8. yes

The States: 1. false; 2. true; 3. false; 4. true; 5. false; 6. true; 7. false; 8. true; 9. true; 10. false

abolish	advice	align

© Carson-Dellosa

biome	caravan	collide

© Carson-Dellosa

depicted	elaborate	epic

© Carson-Dellosa

epicenter	fabric	famished
© Carson-Dellosa	© Carson-Dellosa	© Carson-Dellosa
fantasy	foliage	generate
© Carson-Dellosa	© Carson-Dellosa	© Carson-Dellosa
geyser	gigantic	grazing
© Carson-Dellosa	© Carson-Dellosa	© Carson-Dellosa

hazardous	immigrant	increment
© Carson-Dellosa	© Carson-Dellosa	© Carson-Dellosa
industrial	inflate	inscription
© Carson-Dellosa	© Carson-Dellosa	© Carson-Dellosa
lunge	luxurious	manor
© Carson-Dellosa	© Carson-Dellosa	© Carson-Dellosa

margin	monotonous	ornate
© Carson-Dellosa	© Carson-Dellosa	© Carson-Dellosa
particle	pendulum	phenomena
© Carson-Dellosa	© Carson-Dellosa	© Carson-Dellosa
physician	porous	prestige
© Carson-Dellosa	© Carson-Dellosa	© Carson-Dellosa

promote	propel	proprietor
© Carson-Dellosa	© Carson-Dellosa	© Carson-Dellosa
province	raze	regulate
© Carson-Dellosa	© Carson-Dellosa	© Carson-Dellosa
revolution	sapling	satellite
© Carson-Dellosa	© Carson-Dellosa	© Carson-Dellosa

sensible	slogan	superb
© Carson-Dellosa	© Carson-Dellosa	© Carson-Dellosa
suspicious	sustain	temperate
© Carson-Dellosa	© Carson-Dellosa	© Carson-Dellosa
tier	tundra	varnish
© Carson-Dellosa	© Carson-Dellosa	© Carson-Dellosa

41
× 8

© Carson-Dellosa

25
× 4

© Carson-Dellosa

50
× 7

© Carson-Dellosa

48
× 10

© Carson-Dellosa

12
× 12

© Carson-Dellosa

111
×   8

© Carson-Dellosa

255
×   3

© Carson-Dellosa

530
×   5

© Carson-Dellosa

120
×   2

© Carson-Dellosa

$3\overline{)72}$

$4\overline{)60}$

$3\overline{)54}$

$6\overline{)480}$

$5\overline{)170}$

$9\overline{)153}$

$12\overline{)240}$

$7\overline{)490}$

$8\overline{)416}$

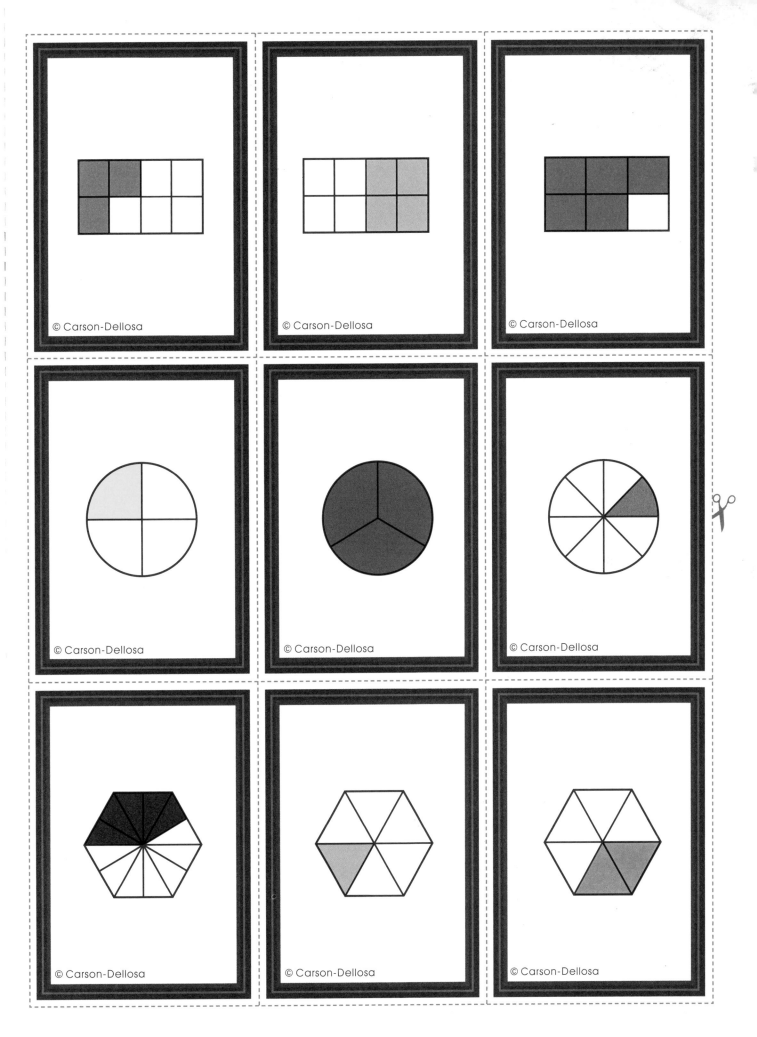

0.8<u>33</u>	0.<u>5</u>	0.37<u>5</u>
© Carson-Dellosa	© Carson-Dellosa	© Carson-Dellosa
0.12<u>5</u>	<u>1</u>	0.<u>25</u>
© Carson-Dellosa	© Carson-Dellosa	© Carson-Dellosa
0.<u>3</u>33	0.1<u>66</u>	0.41<u>66</u>
© Carson-Dellosa	© Carson-Dellosa	© Carson-Dellosa

angle	circumference	degree
© Carson-Dellosa	© Carson-Dellosa	© Carson-Dellosa
diameter	parallel lines	perpendicular lines
© Carson-Dellosa	© Carson-Dellosa	© Carson-Dellosa
radius	ray	segment
© Carson-Dellosa	© Carson-Dellosa	© Carson-Dellosa

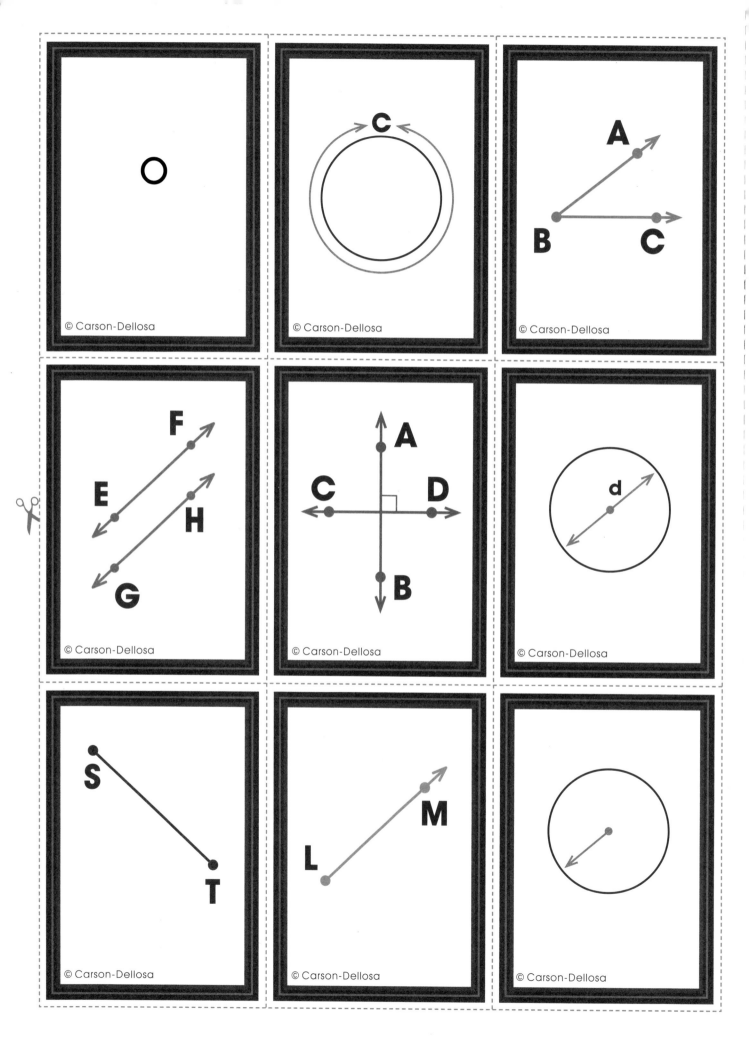

© Carson-Dellosa

© Carson-Dellosa

© Carson-Dellosa

© Carson-Dellosa

© Carson-Dellosa

© Carson-Dellosa

© Carson-Dellosa

© Carson-Dellosa

© Carson-Dellosa

VI	IX	XVI
© Carson-Dellosa	© Carson-Dellosa	© Carson-Dellosa
LVII	CCLXI	DCCVII
© Carson-Dellosa	© Carson-Dellosa	© Carson-Dellosa
MDLX	MMCXV	MCLXXV
© Carson-Dellosa	© Carson-Dellosa	© Carson-Dellosa

$4 + (8 \times 3)$

© Carson-Dellosa

$27 - (24 \div 3)$

© Carson-Dellosa

$(7 \times 5) + 11$

© Carson-Dellosa

$(9 \times 5) - 14$

© Carson-Dellosa

$60 - (30 \div 2)$

© Carson-Dellosa

$22 + (11 \times 2)$

© Carson-Dellosa

$(6 \times 7) - 40$

© Carson-Dellosa

$64 - (8 \times 7)$

© Carson-Dellosa

$63 + (72 \div 8)$

© Carson-Dellosa

The Original
Summer Bridge Activities™

Congratulations!

This certifies that

_____
Name

has completed **Summer Bridge Activities**™.

_____
Parent's Signature

www.carsondellosa.com